Stefania Belloni

CITIES OF ITALY

LUCCA

GUIDE WITH TOWN PLAN

Published and printed by

NARNI - TERNI

LUCCA OVER THE CENTURIES:
The history of the town and its architecture

Lucca is one of the few towns which the visitor can get to know well simply by walking through its streets and squares, because its history is inextricably linked to the continual process of architectural transformation which it has undergone over the centuries, and which a sharp eye is still able to trace.

In every corner of the town we can read a chapter of its life; its walls and churches, its squares and houses, its main shopping street ..... they all talk to us, telling us the story of the past, if only we are willing to stop and listen to them.

The origins of Lucca stretch into to the shadows of time; traces of human settlements dating as far back as the Stone Age have been found in the area. The town was actually ·founded, however, by the Ligurians, followed by the Etruscans and later the Romans, who made it into a stronghold in the 3rd century BC.

The town became a Latin colony in 180 BC, presiding over a prevalently mountainous territory inhabited by the Apuan Ligurians. It was a time of splendour for Lucca; not only was it situated on a geographically strategic spot, it was also close to many important roads like the Cassia, the Aurelia and the Clodia.

From the Roman era, the town still retains its geometrical street-plan, similar to a chessboard, and the area of the Forum, which in Roman times was situated at the intersection between the main North-South street or "cardo maximus" and the main East-West street or "decumanus maximus". St. Michael's Church now stands on this spot. The area occupied by the arena of the Roman amphitheatre is also still visible, though the structure of the amphitheatre is almost completely hidden, as buildings from subsequent periods of time have been constructed over it, in successive layers.

During the barbarian invasions, Lucca was an important military centre and road junction. The Goths endured a long, hard siege at the hands of the Byzantines in the town, and the Lombards made it into the capital of the region of Tuscia, a role it kept until Tuscany became a marquisate in the 9th century.

After many struggles to free itself of feudal domination, in 1162 Lucca was recognized at last as a free city-state by Emperor Frederick I. The town enhanced its prestige further by taking part in the Crusades, and in the 13th century, it became extremely wealthy thanks to its flourishing banking and manufacturing enterprises and its intense trading activity not only with Europe but also with the East. At the same time it was the undisputed capital of the silk industry.

Evidence of this prosperity can be seen in the hundreds of brick houses which were built at this time, each with its own tower crowned with a holm-oak tree. These houses were supported by solid stone pillars and arches which formed ground-level porticos, and were distinguished by mullioned windows with their slender white marble columns. The so-called "tower-houses" date from this period; the streets in the town centre were extremely narrow and there was an increasingly large number of houses crowded together, so houses had to be developed upwards, in towers, rather than horizontally.

Another sign of the town's wealth in

this period was the re-building of the major churches, such as St. Martin's and St. Michael's, which were enlarged and embellished and given splendid Romanesque façades.

But all the wealth and splendour acquired by the town were soon undermined by squabbles and rivalry between its families, which in time developed into a struggle for power between opposing groups such as that between the Guelphs and Ghibellines, and between the Whites and Blacks.

Lucca was later governed by several "Signorie" or feudal lordships, first under Uguccione della Faggiola then, from 1316 to 1328, by Castruccio Castracani, under whom both the area around Luni and the whole of west Tuscany from Volterra to Pistoia were annexed to Lucca. This was followed by a period of bloody civil strife which made the town an easy prey for the Pisans. It was only with the intervention of Charles IV of Bohemia that the town gained its freedom once more in 1369.

For the first thirty years of the 15th century, Lucca was the feudal lordship of Paolo Guinigi. Evidence of his rule remains today in the splendid forms of Palazzo Guinigi in the town centre, of Villa Guinigi, which was originally situated outside the town walls and now houses the National Museum, and in one of the most beautiful and moving sculptures of the whole of the 15th century: the tomb of Guinigi's wife, Ilaria del Carretto, carved by Jacopo

della Quercia, which is kept inside the Cathedral.

After the fall of the Guinigi family, the Republic of Lucca went through alternating periods of good and bad fortune, due mostly to its proximity to the powerful city of Florence. It succeeded in consolidating its position, however, during the 15th and 16th centuries, when it devoted its efforts to preserving its independence, by building, for example, a new circle of walls which would provide the town with a more effective defence from external attacks. But this led to a certain isolation of Lucca from the outside world, and the business classes withdrew from trade and banking activities and invested instead in agriculture.

As a result of this tendency to close in on itself and to operate exclusively on its own territory, the 16th century was a period of intense building in Lucca; the construction of large mansions changed the town's appearance radically, while the surrounding country was transformed by the building of magnificent country houses.

The appearance of the town was completely altered; houses were joined together, towers were partially or fully demolished and new mansions built in their place, inspired by Florentine or Emilian taste. All the most important families changed their homes, remaining inside the town, however, so as to confirm the continuation of their power.

All of the 17th and most of the 18th centuries were characterized by a policy of conservation which underlined the isolation of the Republic of Lucca from developments in Europe, but on 22 January 1799, the old aristocratic republic fell into the hands of Napoleon's troops with hardly any resistance. In the following twelve years of the

Napoleonic Republic of Lucca and of the reign of Napoleon's sister, Elisa, wife of Felice Baciocchi, the town once more underwent considerable architectural changes; many religious buildings were used for public and administrative purposes and the Palazzo Pubblico, in which the Elders who governed the town used to meet, became the residence of the Baciocchi, who also had the large Piazza Napoleone designed in front of the palace.

Abandoned by the French in 1814, on the fall of the Napoleonic Empire, Lucca was handed over to the Bourbon Duchess Maria Luisa of Parma by the Congress of Vienna. The period between 1817 and 1847 was a time of growth and cultural development for the small duchy, as the presence of a court roused the town from the torpor which had isolated it until then. The work of the architect Lorenzo Nottolini dates from this period; he de-signed new plans for several districts and squares in the town and created the delightful walk on top of the town walls. Maria Luisa's son, Carlo Ludovico, continued his mother's work, giving his support to the embellishment of the façades of various buildings and to many other improvements, such as the completion of the Guamo aqueduct by Lorenzo Nottolini and the embankment of the River Serchio.

When Lucca was handed over to the Grand Duchy of Tuscany in 1847, it was in a vulnerable position for having been isolated around court life for too long, and the change proved to be a hard blow. Being incorporated into a much larger state prevented it from finding its identity, and until it was annexed to the Kingdom of Italy, it was practically abandoned to its own resources, and very little new building or improvements of public utility were undertaken.

THE WALLS AND GATES OF LUCCA

THE ROMAN PERIOD

In the Roman period, Lucca was defended by a quadrangle of regular walls eight or nine metres high, made up of limestone blocks. Only a few remains of this first set of walls are still visible, inside the Church of Our Lady of the Rose and just outside it.

The four gates in the Roman walls were: the east gate, later called *Porta San Gervasio* (pointing towards Florence and Rome), the north gate, which was to become *Porta San Frediano* (pointing towards Parma), the west gate, later named *Porta San Donato* (pointing towards Luni) and the south gate, which became *Porta San Pietro* (pointing towards Pisa).

For security reasons, each of the four gates had a postern (a concealed door for emergencies).

THE MEDIEVAL PERIOD

A second set of walls was built around Lucca in the 12th and 13th centuries to include the districts of the churches of Our Lady Outside the Walls, St Pietro Somaldi and St. Frediano. The walls were made up of square stones in even rows; they were approximately 11-12 metres high, defended by crenellated towers and complete with a drawbridge and enormous wooden doors.

Two of the four gates still remain today: Porta San Gervasio, with a single high archway, and Porta Santa Maria dei Borghi, with two archways. The remains of these walls are grandiose, and are evidence of how Lucca must have flourished in the Middle Ages, thanks to the wealth it created from its trade, its banking activity and its silk production.

A third set of walls was completed later, built at different moments in time and by different architects, who limited themselves merely to enlarging the existing perimeter of walls (which is still the same today), and building large circular keeps to the south and the west.

FROM THE 16TH CENTURY TILL TODAY

From the 16th century onwards, the Republic financed further work on the fortifications (to which many private citizens also contributed), supervised by a special Fortifications Office, set up in 1518. A large number of engineers were involved in the first works, but they did not follow a unified plan, which resulted in changes being made to the part of the walls that had already been built. It was not until the end of the century that another group of engineers gave the walls their present, typically Italian, ramparted appearance. By 1645 the circle was almost complete, the finishing touches were entrusted to Paolo Lipparelli and the whole project was finished in 1650. In their definitive form, the walls are 4.2 kilometres long, made up of eleven sections, ten bastions and a platform (St Frediano). The bastions jut a long way out from the sections of wall, and they are all provided with underground rooms for ammunition and food stores; access to them was by a flight of steps on the inside of the walls or by spiral staircases leading directly down into them from the bastions.

On the outside of the walls there was an impressive defensive system, comprising a 35-metre moat, an embankment which defended

The Walls.
*Gate in walls named **Porta San Pietro.***

the road outside the walls and twelve ravelins, or outworks, standing on brickwork bases (two of which are still visible today on the north side).

The various gates in the walls are all of a different style, due to the fact they were designed in different periods of time, by engineers belonging to different cultural backgrounds.

Porta San Pietro (St Peter's Gate) was completed in 1566 and was designed by Alessandro Resta. Above the entrance arch he placed an image of St. Peter and above that he inscribed the coat-of-arms of the Republic of Lucca with its motto "Libertas". The side passages in the gateway were added much later, in 1864.

Porta Santa Maria (Our Lady's Gate) was built in 1593 with a single archway; it was designed by Ginese Bresciani, who decorated it with a marble sculpture of the Madonna and Child. On either side there are two panthers bearing the coat-of-arms of Lucca; these replaced the two lions which the architect had put in his plans and which the Senate had expressly asked to be replaced. The two side archways have only been opened recently.

Porta San Donato (St Donato's Gate) dates from a later period; it was in fact only begun by Muzio Oddi in 1629. Designed in brickwork, it is embellished with elegant marble strips and squares. In comparison with the gate which existed before it, this gate is situated a long way in front of it, as it was at this point that the town expanded, and the walls were built further out compared to the previous ones.

The previous gate, built in 1589 by Vincenzo Vitali, can now be seen in the middle of Piazzale San Donato.

The fourth gate, called Porta Elisa (Elisa's Gate) dates from 1804, and was built in neoclassical style at the wish of Elisa Baciocchi, Napoleon's sister, who wanted to make an opening in the city walls to the east, on the site of the old Roman "decumanus maximus", which had been blocked off in the 16th century for defensive reasons.

The other two gates which can be found along the perimeter of the walls today are Porta Sant'Anna (St Anne's Gate) and Porta San Jacopo (St James' Gate), both of recent construction.

As a matter of fact, the walls have never actually had to defend Lucca from its enemies. The only serious enemy to have threatened the town is the River Serchio when, in 1812, the water level rose to a dangerous height and Lucca risked being flooded. On that occasion, the mighty doors were closed hermetically, allowing Lucca to remain dry.

During the reign of Maria Luisa, in the first half of the 19th century, the Royal Architect, Lorenzo Nottolini, was commissioned to transform the walls, making them into a sort of park accessible from all parts of town. With his usual taste and simplicity, Nottolini made the route along the top of the perimeter of the walls into a shady walk. The walk provides a delightful experience which the visitor should not miss, with its beautiful, centuries-old trees which create shade in summer and the wide range of views it offers, not only of the town centre but also of the Pisa mountains to the south, of the Apuan Alps to the west, of Bagni di Lucca and the Garfagnana mountains to the north, and of the famous country houses to the east.

Gate in walls named **Porta Santa Maria**.
Detail of Porta Santa Maria - panther with the coat-of-arms of Lucca.

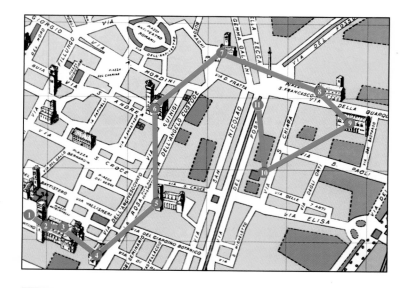

1) PIAZZA S. MARTINO

Piazza San Martino, or Cathedral Square, together with the adjacent square, Piazza Antelminelli, form a corner of great charm and architectural harmony thanks to their spaciousness, the beautiful houses and buildings which stand in them and the fountain situated in the second square. Several architectural styles and periods are represented here. *Palazzo Bernardi* (or *Micheletti*), designed by Ammannati in 1556, is a simple and sober example of early mannerism. The *Cathedral Museum*, on the other hand, dates from the 13th century and is a typical example of medieval architecture in Lucca, with its use of varied building materials, stone arches and mullioned windows with three lights, set inside round arches. The simple *fountain* designed by Lorenzo Nottolini in 1832 and consisting in a single circular basin, fits harmoniously into this corner of the town.

❧⚜❧

2) CATHEDRAL

The *Cathedral*, also called San Martino or St. Martin's, is undoubtedly the most important religious symbol of the town. The story of its construction is a complex one, as it was rebuilt and altered many times over the course of time, but it is interesting because it exemplifies the architectural "stratifications" which many buildings in Lucca were subject-

The Cathedral

ed to over the centuries.
It was St. Frediano who first thought of building a church on this spot, in the 6th century AD. He wished to build a magnificent church dedicated to St. Martin, but unfortunately we can only guess what it must have looked like, because since it became a bishop's see in the 8th century, the church was rebuilt and extended several times.

This happened the first time at the wish of Pope Alexander II, who started again from the foundations in order to have a church built with five naves. The church was consecrated in 1070, in the presence of Matilde of Canossa, but little remains of it to be seen today. The subsequent renovations which took place in the 12th and 13th centuries gave the church an austere Romanesque appearance whereas later reconstruction work, carried out in the 14th and 15th centuries, were in the Gothic style.

THE FAÇADE

The asymmetrical Romanesque façade in marble, which reminds the visitor of Pisa Cathedral in the way it becomes progressively narrower towards the top, and in its rows of numerous slender columns, was built over an existent façade dating from the 11th century.

It dates from 1204, as can be seen in an inscription over one of the upper columns, and was designed by Guidetto da Como. Unlike its Pisan model, however, the slender columns are all carved in different ways (some are carved over their whole surface, others in a spiral or knotted pattern, others in white and green checks, others with a herring-bone motif .....), and are made out of white and green marble. The other decorative features of the façade include coats-of-arms, rosettes, animal and plant sculptures, figures and

"READING" A CHURCH

For those who know how to read it, the history of a town is often written within the walls of its cathedral. A cathedral represents the wealth of a community because in its naves and on its altars and walls, historical relics and souvenirs of the heroic deeds of its citizens are kept, the remains of its most significant personalities and saints are preserved, and the artists who visited the town leave the evidence of their talent. At the same time, a cathedral houses the most precious craftwork produced by the town, together with objects brought by travellers from distant lands.

The abilities and skills of a community are all recorded inside the cathedral. It is for this reason that we do not only find sacred themes in the works of art kept inside a cathedral, but also allegorical and symbolic motifs, and depictions of the community's legends, traditions and customs. Every feature and peculiarity of the town is recorded in its cathedral, ennobled by being kept in a holy place.

We should try to understand the meaning of a cathedral for the members of a community: for them it not only represents the occasion in which they unite with God in each other's presence, but it also has a highly civic significance as the expression of the community and its history.

A cathedral, especially if it dates from the Romanesque period, is rarely the expression and work of a single generation; it is an integral part of the history of the town and as such, it belongs not only to the present but to the past and to the future.

The collective and choral expression of a community, the cathedral is passed down from one generation to the next, whether in a completed state or not, so that each generation can add its contribution and leave its own mark on it.

The visitor should not be preoccupied, therefore, with being able to identify the stylistic unity of a cathedral; it is far more important to discover the feeling of continuity and cooperation in the work of those who, century after century, have contributed to the development of the community and its religious symbol in harmony with the work of those who preceded them.

View of Piazza San Martino from the Cathedral portico. The 13th century building which now houses the Cathedral Museum can also be seen.

patterns carved in the space above the arches, which later were to inspire the precious fabrics produced by craftsmen in the town.

The upper part of the façade is unfinished; a final row of arches and the tympanum are missing. If it had been completed, it would probably have been very similar to St. Michael's, and the façade would have been higher than the body of the church.

The deep portico with its three large arches and, above it, the three rows of blind arches and slender columns which form three narrow loggias, are typical of the Lombard Romanesque style and create a delightful contrast of light and shade, giving an impression of depth and upward movement. The archway on the right-hand side is noticeably smaller than the one on the left, because room had to be left for the pre-existing bell tower. There is just one sculpture on the marble brackets on the outside wall between the archways: it portrays St. Martin with the Poor Man and is the cement cast of the original which is kept inside the Cathedral.

THE PORTICO

Inside the portico, the three lunettes above the entrance-doors immediately catch the eye: in the centre there is an Ascension attributed to a sculptor from Lombardy known as the "Maestro Lombardo", who worked in Lucca in the 13th century, and who probably also sculpted both the right-hand lunette, portraying the

Panels with episodes from the life of St. Martin and the Months of the Year.

Martyrdom of St. *Regolo,* and the lintel above the right-hand door depicting St. *Regolo's Dispute.* The lintel above the central door portrays *Mary and the Apostles* and is

The carved labyrinth inside the portico reminds us of the labyrinth built by Dedalus, as the Latin inscription tells us.

the work of Guido Bigarelli, who also designed the portico and decorated the doorways. The left-hand lunette contains a real masterpiece: a D*eposition* by Nicola Pisano. This artist from the Apulia region, the "heel" of Italy, worked in Lucca in the first half of the 13th century; he had already assimilated the new Gothic style and used this commission as an opportunity to work in a radically innovative way. His sculpture is therefore characterized by Gothic elements, including the introduction of realism in the depiction of divine subjects. We should keep this in mind as we observe the human suffering depicted with intensity in the figures he carved; their deep wrinkles express the tragedy of the event, and the way they are massed together and bent over, as if crushed by the curving arch of the lunette, accen-

In the lunette above the central doorway, Ascension of Christ between Two Angels ("Maestro Lombardo", 13th century). The lintel portrays Mary and the Twelve Apostles.

tuates the drama of the scene.

The lintel beneath the lunette is also the work of Nicola Pisano, representing the *Annunciation, Nativity* and *Adoration of the Magi.*

At the sides of the central doorway there are carved panels containing *episodes from the life of St. Martin* and below them are scenes depicting the *twelve months of the year,* with the *signs of the zodiac* beside them; these are probably the work of the "Maestro Lombardo". There is also a *labyrinth* carved on the pillar next to the bell tower; the Latin inscription informs us that no-one can find their way out of the labyrinth built by Dedalus of Crete except for the Greek Theseus, thanks to Ariadne's thread.

THE INTERIOR

The Cathedral is a treasure-trove of precious and important works

of art.

The interior is unique in its kind in Lucca, being the only church with a vaulted ceiling whereas nearly all the other churches in the town have ceilings supported by a triangular structure of beams. The plan is prevalently Romanesque, with the occasional touch of Gothic influence; the interior is in the form of a Latin cross and is divided into three naves and a transept, itself made up of two naves and a semicircular apse.

Evidence of the Gothic style, which established itself towards the end of the 14th century, can be seen in the graceful row of pointed, mullioned windows in the women's gallery, built above and along the central nave as far as the transept.

As we enter, the first marble sculpture which we meet on the inside wall of the façade is of St. *Martin with the Poor Man*, dating from the 13th century and attributed to the "Maestro Lombardo". There are also two holy-water basins carved by Matteo Civitali in 1498, placed near two pillars which mark the beginning of the central nave.

Civitali also carved the pulpit and designed the splendid inlaid white and green marble floor, with its geometrical patterns which divide up the surface of the nave floors in such a beautifully-proportioned and attractive way. Along the right nave, above the second altar we can see *The Adoration of the Magi* by Federico Zuccari, and on the third altar we can admire a painting which makes a great impact with its chiaroscuro and colour effects: *The Last Supper*, painted specially by Tintoretto in 1590 for this altar. The unusual perspective, the ele-

Magnificent view of the interior of the Cathedral.

vated position of Christ and the crowding of the figures around him give the painting enormous dramatic intensity.

In the right transept there are two *monumental tombs* by Matteo Civitali, one in commemoration of Domenico Bertini, a well-known patron of the town, dated 1479, and the other commemorating Pietro di Noceto, dated 1472, which according to records passed down to us was evaluated by Antonio Rossellini as worth 450 golden ducats. In the adjacent Chapel of the Sacrament, two delicate *adoring angels* are also the work of Civitali. St. R*egolo's altar*, the large altar at the end of the right nave, dates back to 1484.

At the sides of the presbytery we can see the fragments of the old choir-stalls in porphyry and serpentine, which was carved in Civitali's workshop; the choir-stalls

In the Cathedral, sculpture of St. Martin with the Poor Man, placed on the inside of the façade (attributed to the "Maestro Lombardo", 13th century).

in the presbytery are 15th century and have been attributed to Marti, the apse is decorated with 17th century frescoes and the stained glass windows are the work of Pandolfo.

In the left transept we find the *Altar of Freedom*, commissioned by the people of Lucca to commemorate their regained freedom in 1369 and to celebrate the greatness of their town; we can see an image of the town, with its new circle of walls, in Giambologna's 16th century bas-relief in the altar panel. Above the altar, which was made by Giambologna's school, is an impressive statue of the *Resurrected Christ* (1577-79), the work of Giambologna himself, whereas the two statues of St. *Peter* and St. *Paolino* are the work of his school.

Not far from the altar stands a statue which was once kept outside the Cathedral: St. *John the Evangelist*, carved by Jacopo della

---

Tintoretto: Last Supper *(circa* 1590), *situated on the third altar on the right.*

Quercia at the beginning of the 15th century.

In the nearby Sanctuary Chapel we will find a precious painting by the Domenican monk Fra Bartolomeo della Porta, an *Enthroned Madonna and Child with St. Stephen and St. John the Baptist*, painted at the beginning of the 16th century. It is a striking picture thanks to its clean lines and intense colours. The placid immobility of the figures conveys a feeling of peace and serene detachment.

At the centre of the transept we will find the famous *Tomb of Ilaria del Carretto*, an inspired work by Jacopo della Quercia, commissioned in 1406 by Paolo Guinigi, Lord of Lucca and Ilaria's husband. The sculpture shows traces of French influence, but also shows classical elements such as the cupids which hold up the garlands around the base of the tomb.

It is considered by unanimous agreement to be the most beautiful tomb to have been made for a woman in the Renaissance period.

In the left nave, an important

Enthroned Madonna and Child with St. Stephen and St. John the Baptist (Fra' Bartolomeo della Porta, 1509) in the Sanctuary Chapel.

ILARIA'S ETERNAL SLEEP

Ilaria del Carretto, second wife of Paolo Guinigi, Lord of Lucca, died very young on 8 December 1405 giving birth to a baby girl, also named Ilaria. Her husband commissioned her tomb from Jacopo della Quercia, who completed it in 1408.

The art historian Vasari, in the second edition of his book *Lives*, comments that the sculptor "........ carved several marble cupids on the base holding a festoon, sculpted with such clarity that they seem to be made of flesh and blood; and on the coffin placed on top of this base, with infinite care he carved the image of Paolo's wife ..... and then she was buried in it". Vasari also mentions another detail of the tomb: "In the same piece of marble he carved a dog with rounded forms, as a symbol of her faithfulness to her husband", thus explaining the sculptor's wish to symbolize Ilaria's wifely virtues through her faithful dog, Diana.

But gentle Ilaria was not destined to rest in peace for long. Paolo Guinigi was driven out of Lucca in 1429, and the tomb was consequently dismantled: a part of it ended up in the sacristy and a part in the Garbesi Chapel, while the panels with the cupids were sent to the Uffizi Gallery in Florence and then to the Bargello Museum. Today we can once more admire the marvellous work in its entirety because it was reassembled and given a permanent place in the centre of the transept in 1889.

Illuminated by the light which enters from outside, the supine figure of the young woman is calm and serene; despite her immobility, she seems ready to wake up from one moment to the next, recalled, perhaps, to life by the barking of her small dog, Diana, who lies at her feet waiting for a sign from her.

Tomb made by Jacopo della Quercia for Ilaria del Carretto, wife of Paolo Guinigi, ruler of Lucca in the early 15th century: possibly the most beautiful tomb ever to have been made for a woman.

monument in the history of the town catches the eye. It is the *Small Temple of the Holy Effigy*, an octagonal structure in Carrara marble, with slabs of red porphyry, designed by Matteo Civitali in 1484 to house the famous wooden crucifix called the *Holy Effigy* or *Holy Cross*. The image of Christ is in polychrome wood but time and candle smoke make it difficult to distinguish the different colours of the various kinds of wood used. According to legend, the crucifix was carved out of a Lebanese cedar by Nicodemus, whose hand was guided by angels, but then it had to be hidden during the persecution of the Christians. Much later it was placed in a boat and entrusted to the open sea, without a guide. It miraculously reached the Mediterranean, after escaping from pirate attacks, and one day it came to land on the shore at

Detail of the Holy Effigy, the wooden sculpture carved out of a cedar by Nicodemus in the Middle Ages.

Luni. In view of the fortuitous way in which the crucifix had reached them, the people who found it decided to entrust it once more to chance, so that its final destination would be chosen by divine will. They loaded it onto a cart driven by wild oxen which, of their own accord, turned towards Lucca. There the Holy Effigy was venerated with increasing devotion, not least because of the many miracles which were attrib-uted to its divine powers. There is, however, another, less roman-ticized version of the origins of this crucifix, according to which it was commissioned by Pope Alexander II from a Lombard artist in the second half of the 11th century, as part of the Pope's plans for a spiritual renewal of the church in Lucca. These two conflicting versions can, however, be reconciled, in that several documents exist which refer to a

Small Temple of the Holy Effigy.

much older Holy Effigy of unknown origin which was kept in St. Martin's before the present one. Every September solemn celebrations are held at Lucca to commemorate the transfer of the Crucifix from St. Frediano's to St. Martin's; for the occasion, the crucifix is covered with precious and elaborate vestments, manufactured by Lucca craftsmen in the 14th and 17th centuries. The altar situated in front of the Crucifix houses a painting by Bronzino dating from 1598, the *Presentation of Mary in the Temple*. As we leave the Cathedral, we must not forget to admire the fresco by Cosimo Rosselli on the inside wall of the façade, depicting some of the most significant episodes of the *Legend of the Holy Effigy*.

THE SACRISTY

Entrance to the sacristy is at the end of the right nave, through a

One of the angels sculpted by Matteo Civitali in the second half of the 15th century.

doorway dating back to the early 15th century, with pillars which reveal the hand of the sculptor Jacopo della Quercia.

Inside the sacristy, there is a splendid picture above the beautiful altar of St. Agnello, depicting an *Enthroned Madonna and Child with Four Saints*, which was painted by Domenico Ghirlandaio between 1449 and 1494. This painting, like all the artist's works, is notable for de-picting, with great accuracy, the characteristics and style of the historical period in which it was painted, thus becoming a record of the habits and usages of its time. Even in his depictions of sacred subjects, Ghirlandaio never failed to portray, in the greatest detail, the style of dress, the fabrics, the decorations in local houses, the architectural features and landscapes of his time, revealing almost a

Resurrected Christ (Giambologna, 1577-79), on the Altar of Freedom.

Flemish taste for accurate detail. The scenes on the altar panel, depicting the lives of saints, were painted by some of Ghirlandaio's pupils and in particular by Bartolomeo di Giovanni. The lunette portraying the *Dead Christ supported by Nicodemus* is attributed to Filippino Lippi. At the sides of the altar there is a triptych with a golden background painted by the Lucca School in the 14th century, and a *Madonna with Angels and Saints* painted by the Florentine School in the 15th century. The *Annunciation* on the north side is by Leonardo Grazia, known as "Il Pistoia", and dates from the first half of the 16th century.

Enthroned Madonna with Four Saints (Ghirlandaio, 1449-1494).

Beautiful sculpture inside the Cathedral.

3) CATHEDRAL MUSEUM

Housed in a mansion of the 13th/14th century, which looks out onto Piazza Antelminelli and is embellished with elegant mullioned windows, the *Cathedral Museum* (Museo dell'Opera del Duomo) contains most of the treasures of the Cathedral, a large number of works of art and the ornaments and vestments belonging not only to the Cathedral but also to the nearby Church of St. John and Reparata. These include a large, finely engraved, silver crucifix from the 14th century known as the *Cross of the Pisans* because according to an anecdote it was stolen from the Pisans. One side of the cross is engraved with saints encircled by a rich profusion of volutes of leaves while the other side is engraved with twenty-four prophets inside the same number of lilies. The cross is exhibited on the main altar in the Cathedral during celebrations in honour of the Holy Cross.

There are many other paintings and sculptures, including the *Apostle* by Jacopo della Quercia and a *Beheaded St. John* attributed to Matteo Civitali. There are also beautifully illustrated books, reliquaries, and the vestments used to cover the Holy Effigy during the celebrations held in its honour.

Cathedral Museum.

Church of Our Lady of the Rose - doorway.

Church of Our Lady of the Rose.

4) CHURCH OF OUR LADY OF THE ROSE

Behind the Cathedral, at the back of the *Palazzo Vescovile* (Bishops' Residence) is the small *Church of Our Lady of the Rose* (Santa Maria della Rosa).

Built in Pisan Gothic style, the church dates back from 1309 and originally was adjacent to an oratory which was then incorporated into the church; we can still see its entrance door and mullioned windows. It was commissioned by the Corporation of Merchants; around 1333 it was enlarged, and the austere Romanesque structure was embellished with the addition of mullioned windows set inside large round arches, which make the building considerably lighter and more graceful, and which are a characteristic feature of the town's medieval architecture. Unfortunately the façade no longer has its outer covering in marble but its doorway, probably the work of Matteo Civitali, can still be admired. The interior is divided into three naves and is from a later period; on the left the remains of a few square stones which were part of the Roman walls in the 2nd century AD are visible.

5) CHURCH OF OUR LADY OUTSIDE THE WALLS

This church (Santa Maria Forisportam, also called Santa Maria Bianca), owes its name to the fact that it was originally situated outside the Roman town walls. It dates back to the end of the 12th century and is an interesting example of the local Romanesque style. The upper part of the façade is in fact decorated with the characteristic rows of loggias in white marble, and below them, in the lower half of the façade, there is a series of blind arches which continue along the side walls, transepts and apse.

The archways enclosing the three doors leading into the church are finely sculpted with figures and ornamental motifs of a classical stamp; the lunettes above the doors depict, on the right, a Bishop dating from the 13th century, on the left an Enthroned Madonna dating from the 17th century, and in the middle another 17th century work, depicting the Crowning of the Virgin. The Romanesque interior is divided into three naves; the central nave and transept were made higher in the 16th century, using brickwork, and then were covered by vaulted arches. The church houses several precious works of art. The *Statue of the Assumption* and the main altar on which it is placed are the work of Matteo Civitali; on the fourth altar on the right there is a fine St. *Lucy* by Guercino and on the altar in the right transept we can admire a 17th century tabernacle. The unusual baptismal font

---

The large square in front of the Church of Our Lady Outside the Walls, with its Roman column, which used to be the finishing-point for the traditional race which took place in the town every year until the end of the 18th century.

was made out of an Early Christian tomb. In the square outside the church, we are struck by the presence of a solitary column; it is a Roman column made of granite which was used until the end of the 18th century as the finishing-point of the traditional race which was run every year in Lucca during the period of the local festival. The 17th century *Palazzo Sirti* designed by Domenico Martelli and *Palazzo Penitesi* which hosted a visit by the French writer Montaigne in 1581 both look out onto the square.

6) GUINIGI TOWN HOUSES AND TOWER

The residential complex of houses belonging to the Guinigi family, a local family of wealthy merchants and bankers, was originally made up of several town houses, towers and loggias. Even today the complex is still a splendid example of medieval architecture of Romanesque and Gothic inspiration, although only one of the four original towers has remained and the

Guinigi Tower.

Palazzo Guinigi - mullioned windows with three and four lights.

loggia and ground-level porticos are now walled in.

This handsome complex was built in brickwork; its salient feature is its ground-floor level, made up of a series of stone arches resting on pillars; the arches were originally open to form porticos. On the upper floors, large trefoil mullioned windows with three or four lights make the red brick walls lighter and more graceful.

The building in the best state of conservation is the one on the corner between Via S. Andrea and Via Guinigi. It belonged to Michele and Francesco Guinigi and is the only one with a tower left standing. The tower has with time become one of the town's symbols and is crowned with luxuriant holm oaks. It is visited by tourists for the panoramic view it affords of the town from the top.

The 13th century *Church of St. Simon and St. Judas* (SS. *Simone e Giuda*) is situated nearby; a jewel of the Romanesque style, this small church has an austere grey stone façade with three doorways and an elegant mullioned window above.

7) CHURCH OF ST. PIETRO SOMALDI

The *Church of St. Pietro Somaldi* was erected the first time during the period of the Lombard domination, and is named after its founder, Sumuald. It was rebuilt at the end of the 12th century, and completed two centuries later. The simple façade, striped with grey sandstone and white limestone, follows the Pisan model with its double rows of arches which become narrower towards the top.

Above the three doorways are decorated lunettes inside arches made of two differently coloured kinds of stone. The lintel above the central doorway is sculpted in great detail; attributed to Guido Bigarelli, it represents the *Handing of the Keys to St. Peter* and dates from 1203.

In the interior, which is divided into three naves, several pictures of the 16th century are kept: an *Assumption* by Zacchia da Vezzano, some portraits of Saints attributed to Raffaellino del Garbo, and other interesting works by Franchi, Landucci and Tofanelli.

In the church square there are several interesting 16th century mansions, including the *Bartolomei - Spada Palaces*. The perimeter of the square, although irregular, gives an impression of harmony, even more so thanks to the presence of a lovely garden and, in springtime, a balcony full of flowers.

Interior of the Church of St. Pietro Somaldi (12th-14th century).

Façade of the Church of St. Pietro Somaldi and the bell tower, built in different periods.
Detail of the central doorway, with a lintel depicting the Handing of the Keys to St. Peter, attributed to Guido Bigarelli (1203).

Façade of the Church of St. Francis.

8) CHURCH OF ST. FRANCIS

St Francis's Church (San Francesco) has a long history of rebuilding and alteration work. It was begun in 1228 but was rebuilt and extended in the following century, and was again altered in the 17th century. The latest work to be carried out on it was quite recent - 1930 - and involved the upper half of the façade. The façade is in white limestone and has two large blind arches and a splayed central doorway, of smaller dimensions. There are two niches on either side of the doorway, one of the 11th and one of the 12th century, which originally housed

tombs. The interior has a ceiling made with a triangular beam structure, a single nave and three chapels in the apse.

Lucca has entrusted a large part of its historical heritage to this church, including the third altar, which was commissioned by the Corporation of Weavers to commemorate the episode of the "Uprising of the Ragamuffins" in 1531, which originated in this part of town. The weavers placed their symbol (a bale of raw silk) on the columns which supported the altar and dedicated their new state of neediness to St. Francis, advocate of poverty, as we can read in the inscription in Latin which commemorates the episode.

A memorial tablet nearby commemorates Castruccio Castracani, who was Lord of Lucca at the end of the 14th century and was a member of the noble Antelminelli family. The tombs of the musicians Luigi Boccherini and Francesco Geminiani are found on the left, between the second and third altars.

In the main chapel, the choir-stalls and lectern date from the 15th century, and are the work of Leonardo Marti. To the right of the tribune there are some frescoes of the Florentine school, from the 15th century, which have been removed from the wall.

The church also has a 13th century sacristy and three cloisters, in which several medieval tombs are preserved.

꧁꧂

9) VILLA GUINIGI

Villa Guinigi is the splendid country house which Paolo Guinigi had built for himself at the beginning of the 15th century outside the town walls, in the period in which he was Lord of Lucca.

Also named *Palazzo dei Borghi*, to distinguish it from his residence in the centre of town, the house was built in brick, which was very expensive at the time, and has two façades; the ground floor is made up of eight open arches which form a portico on one side, and seven arches on the other side. The architectural style of the building is not dissimilar to that of the Guinigi town houses; here too, we find the characteristic trefoil mullioned windows supported by slender, white marble columns and set in round arches. The materials used - red brick, white marble, and grey stone for the pillars - are also the same as those used in the town. There are no exact records of the architects who worked on the building, but it is thought that the builders were probably from the North of Italy, who were specialized in the typical Romanesque-Gothic style

Villa Guinigi.

which was fashionable in Lucca at the time.

What distinguishes this building from others of the same period is its grandiose size, the regular lines of the walls and the spaciousness of the portico. The garden, which was once enclosed inside a crenellated wall, has only been partly preserved, but we can trace its original boundaries in the structure of the streets in the vicinity.

Today Villa Guinigi houses the National Museum, after re-structuring work carried out according to the most modern criteria in exhibition design, which has transformed it into a museum of the highest standard.

NATIONAL MUSEUM IN VILLA GUINIGI

The Museum contains, almost exclusively, works commissioned by individuals, authorities and associations belonging to Lucca, and which have been gathered together from churches, palaces and private collections. By visiting the Museum we can trace most of the intense and extremely rich art history of the town, which has developed over a span of a thousand years.

GROUND FLOOR
Archaeological finds
The ground floor houses exhibits ranging from the prehistoric to the late Roman period, including objects found in various Etruscan and Ligurian tombs, a sacrificial altar recently

---

Columns and capitals (11th century).

Madonna and Child (Matteo Civitali).

unearthed in Piazza San Michele, a large number of Roman inscriptions, mosaics from the 1st century AD and a fragment of Roman wall, made out of tufa, next to the entrance.

Medieval art

Here we can admire sculptures, bas-reliefs and precious wooden objects, from the Romanesque, Gothic and early Renaissance periods.

Two tomb-stones are worth noting in the south gallery: that of Balduccio Parghia degli Antelminelli, ascribed to Jacopo della Quercia, and that of Caterina degli Antelminelli, carved by his school.

The finely-sculpted 13th century columns which originally belonged to the façade of the Church of St. Michael in the Forum are also worth noting, for their splendid embroidery-like animal and flower decorations which reveal the influence of Benedetto Antelami's school.

The Romanesque works which can be seen in Room III are interesting, including the high relief of *Samson fighting with the lion* by a Lucca sculptor of the 13th century, kept originally in the Cathedral, and a series of capitals, statues, ambos and panels from the 8th to the 14th centuries.

In Room V there is a bas-relief of a *Madonna with Child* in gilded and painted marble, attributed to Matteo Civitali, which used to embellish the Merchants' Loggia, that no longer exists.

IST FLOOR

Room X contains some fine works in inlaid wood; to be admired in particular is the multi-coloured marquetry of Cristoforo Canozzi da Lendinara (15th century) in the doors of the cupboard from St. Martin's sacristy. There is a series of precious painted and carved crosses from the 12th and 13th centuries, including one by Berlinghiero and one by Orlandi. In Room XII, there is an unusual 14th century tabernacle by Priamo della Quercia, Jacopo's brother. Room XIII is interesting for its paintings of various schools including those of Botticelli and Filippino Lippi. There are also several works by the "Master of the Lathrop Tondo", who was given this name because he acquired his style from studying the Guinigi Tondo in the Lathrop Collection. His painting shows Flemish inspiration, as well as the influence of Ghirlandaio and

View of town (15th century engraving).

Filippino Lippi.
Room XIV contains several altarpieces, masterpieces by Fra Bar-

One of the rooms in the National Museum.

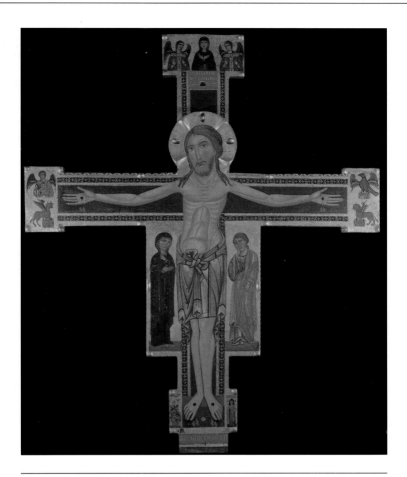

Crucifix with episodes from the Passion of Christ (Berlinghiero, 13th century).

tolomeo from the first half of the 16th century: *The Eternal Father appearing to St. Mary Magdalene and to St. Catherine* and *Our Lady of Mercy*. In the other rooms there are church ornaments and vestments, examples of the famous, precious cloth weaved by Lucca craftsmen between the 16th and 18th centuries, and clothes and jewels from the Lombard era.

Rooms XVI - XVII house paintings from the 17th and 18th centuries, including works by Pietro Paolini (*The Martyrdom of St. Bartholomew*,

The Martyrdom of St. Ponziano and *The Birth of St. John the Baptist*, to mention a few), who worked in Lucca in the second half of the 17th century and was strongly influenced by Caravaggio, and others by Pompeo Batoni, dating from the 18th century (including his famous portrait of *The Archbishop Giovan Domenico Mansi*, painted in 1765, and *The Ecstasy of St. Catherine*). There are also paintings by Guido Reni, Girolamo Scaglia and Lanfranco and Pietro da Cortona.

Madonna and Child with St.Sebastian and St.Rocco (Zacchia the Elder).

Eternal Father with St. Mary Magdalene and St. Catherine of Siena (Fra' Bartolomeo, 1509).

Madonna and Child (Ugolino Lorenzetti, 14th century).
Wrought iron strong-box (16th century).

Portrait of Archbishop Giovan Domenico Mansi (Pompeo Batoni, 18th century).

Column of the Madonna dello Stellario (G. Lazzoni di Carrara, 1687).

10) VILLA BUONVISI

Villa Buonvisi, also known as Villa Bottini, together with Villa Guinigi, are the only country houses to be found today inside the town walls.

Villa Buonvisi is considered a perfect example of Renaissance architecture in Lucca.

Three different architects were involved in the design of the building: one is the main architect, whose name is not known to us; one is Vincenzo Civitali, who designed the doorway and windows in the walls surrounding the garden; the third is Buontalenti, who designed the unusual entrance to the nymphaeum at the bottom of the garden, made up of four pairs of columns and a balustrade decorated with two statues symbolizing rivers. These are the only remains left of the original structures of the garden, which was so well known in its time that the name of Buonvisi was for a time synonymous with the name for a garden.

Several rooms inside the house are decorated with a series of frescoes depicting mythological and allegorical scenes, painted by Ventura Salimbeni, a 16th century artist from Siena.

❧

11)VIA DEI FOSSI (CANAL STREET)

This street takes its name from the canal which runs along the centre of it. Two thirds of the street follow the line of the medieval town walls of which the old *Gate of San Gervasio e Protasio*, commonly known as the *Portone dell'Annunziata*, remains, made of grey sandstone with white limestone strips.

On the bridge in front of the gate, there is a small neoclassical marble fountain, one of the many designed at the same time by Lorenzo Nottolini and placed in various spots around the town. The fountain was meant to distribute water brought into the town by the Guamo aqueduct, another of Nottolini's projects just outside Lucca, made up of a long series of arches which linked the Hill of Guamo to the town.

At the end of the street there is a column of the *Madonna dello Stellario*, erected in 1687 by Giovanni Lazzoni. On the base of the column is a fine view of Lucca of the time in bas-relief; we can see St. *Donato's Gate*, a drawbridge and the ravelins in front of the ramparts; these were already covered with leafy trees.

View of Via dei Fossi.

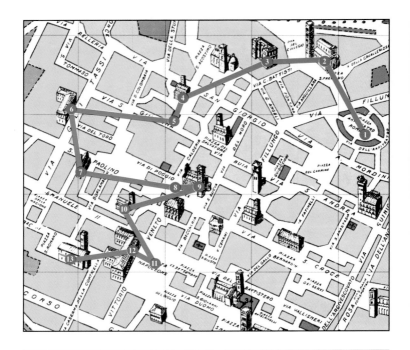

1) PIAZZA DEL MERCATO

If we did not know that Piazza del Mercato stands on the area occupied in the past by the arena of the Roman amphitheatre, we would think that the architect Lorenzo Nottolini had used his imagination to design a curiously-shaped square. But actually Nottolini, who was commissioned by the Bourbon Duke Carlo Ludovico in 1830 to create harmony out of the heterogeneous buildings grouped in a random manner on the foundations of the Roman am-

phitheatre, simply levelled the existent square and opened up the road which once led inside the amphitheatre, thus creating the delightful and highly original square which we still find there today.

Nottolini wanted to preserve the uninterrupted curving line of the houses which stood on the edges of the arena, but had the houses standing in the middle of it knocked down and the surface of the square levelled.

At the same time, he preserved the different heights of the houses standing around the square,

Some of the buildings in Piazza del Mercato, also called Piazza dell'Anfiteatro.

obtaining a charming effect with these few simple operations.

The original level of the amphitheatre is three metres below the ground, buried underneath the series of houses built on top of it in successive centuries. The amphitheatre was built by the Romans just outside their town walls between the 1st and 3rd centuries AD.

It could accommodate a large number of spectators - up to 10,000 - on 24 tiers supported by pilasters; above the tiers, there were two rows of fifty-four arches placed one on top of the other.

Originally lined in marble and embellished by columns, the amphitheatre was abandoned during the barbaric invasions, and gradually became a source of high-quality building materials, especially for the construction of religious and civic buildings in the town.

With time, a large number of houses was built on the solid foundations of the amphitheatre, and in this way the elliptical form of the arena was preserved.

The only original parts of the amphitheatre which can still be seen today are on the east side, including the original entrance archway; the other archways leading into the square today date from the last century.

2) CHURCH OF ST. FREDIANO

The "basilica Langobardorum" commissioned by Bishop Frediano in the 6th century and dedicated to St. Vincent, is the original structure on which the present church of St. Frediano was built.

The church was dedicated to St.

White marble façade of the Church of St. Frediano.

Frediano by his successor, Bishop John, who also had Frediano's tomb placed in the crypt. Bishop John was one of the first to plan the reconstruction of the church, which was to be rebuilt and altered several times over the centuries; in the 12th century, for example, it was modified to face in a different direction, and in the 13th century the building was made three metres higher, which led to alterations in the apse and façade.

The church took on its present appearance in the 16th century, when neighbouring buildings were incorporated into it and several chapels were built along its side walls.

THE FAÇADE

Simple but striking, with its handsome mosaic portraying the *Ascension of Christ*, the façade is a significant example of Romanesque architecture in Lucca.

Its surface, lined with white marble, easily catches the light, and is decorated by architectural details such as the buttresses, which mark the internal division of the church into three naves, and the mosaic, which is almost suspended at the top of the façade, and is supported by a row of columns underneath it.

The mosaic, Byzantine in style, dates from the 13th century and is the work of Berlinghiero. The central figure of Christ, flanked by two angels who carry him upwards as the Apostles watch, is solemn and detached from what is happening, reflecting to perfection the characteristics of religious spirituality and eternity which the Byzantine style favoured. There are three very simple doorways into the church; above the central door is a fine 12th century lintel, the only decoration on the lower part of the façade.

Ascension of Christ in the 13th century mosaic by Berlinghiero's school.

THE INTERIOR

The interior is without a doubt one of the finest expressions of 13th century Italian architecture. The central nave, with its two impressive rows of columns, is solemn and lofty. Way above the columns, the part of the walls added in the 13th century to increase the height of the church can be seen, resting on a simple ledge and divided up by large, classical-style windows.

The apse is illuminated with the light from two rows of windows and is quite austere, its only embellishment being a simple gallery.

At the sides of the central nave there are two smaller naves and a long series of side chapels added in different centuries.

The first work of art to be admired is the *baptismal font* which is situated on the right on entering the church. Made up of a large circular bowl decorated on the outside with bas-reliefs, it contains a central basin, crowned with a carved lid resting on small columns. It dates back to the mid 12th century and was the work of several artists, including the sculptor known as the "Maestro Lombardo", who was certainly responsible for the carving of the *Stories of Moses*. The figures, depicted with vigorous simplicity, crowd together in four of the six panels of the font in unbroken succession, creating a vivid and uninterrupted sequence of events, and they seem to anticipate the work of Nicola Pisano. The *Crossing of the Red Sea* is of particular interest, depicting the Pharaoh's soldiers wearing medieval clothes and armaments.

The figures of the *Good Shepherd* and the *Six Prophets* carved on the two remaining panels are ascribed to a different sculptor, who signed his name on the edge of the font with the following inscription: "Me fecit Robertus magister in arte peritus". The marked Byzantine style and the slight figures, set inside delicate arches reminiscent of Roman decorations, distinguish this work clearly from that of the sculptor of the Stories of Moses.

The decoration of the basin inside the font is the work of a third artist. The basin is embellished with large masks from which water flows. The high, sloping lid is decorated with sculptures depicting, above, the *Apostles*, and below, the symbols of the *Months*,

Interior of Church of St. Frediano - Romanesque baptismal font decorated with splendid bas-reliefs.

while the pillar which supports the basin depicts, in a stylized way, water flowing. This third sculptor has a classical style which distinguishes him from the other two.

On the wall behind the baptismal font there is a large lunette in glazed terracotta by Andrea della Robbia, depicting the *Annunciation*.

The adjacent Fatinelli Chapel, built in the 17th century, contains pictures by Guidotti and Tintore. The latter painted episodes from the life of St. Zita, whose tomb and preserved body can be seen in the chapel.

THE LEGEND OF ST. ZITA

"…. he held a sinner by both his hips
clutching him by the tendons of his feet.
From our bridge he said: " O evil-claws,
here is one of the Elders of St. Zita!
Throw him in, and I'll go back again
to that town which is full of them:
every man there is corrupt, apart from Bontura,
and a no becomes a yes for money there."

Dante - Inferno - Canto XXI

From the words Dante uses to describe one of the sinners he meets in hell, a certain Martino Bottaio, whom he holds up as an example of the corruption among the magistrates of Lucca, it is obvious that he did not have a good opinion of Lucca's middle classes in the late thirteenth/early fourteenth century. But it is not so much his opinion of the people of Lucca that interests us so much here as the fact that already in Dante's time, St Zita was synonymous with Lucca, and the name of the saint was indissolubly linked to the name of her home-town. Dante knew therefore that St. Zita was dear to the people of Lucca, but where did so much devotion come from?

We know that the pious woman lived in the 13th century in Lucca, where she was a servant in the house of the noble Fantinelli family. Her position allowed her to do charitable works among the poor in the town, by taking bread and other food from the well-supplied pantry of the house and distributing it to the needy.

Legend has it that one day her master saw her as she was taking some bread to the poor. When he asked her what was in her bulging apron, she replied there were roses and flowers. Her master was suspicious and insisted on checking it was true; in the meantime, the bread she was carrying to the poor had miraculously become roses and flowers.

This was not the only miracle she worked, but every year the people of Lucca still commemorate that particular miracle, celebrating the anniversary every April by blessing the daffodils in bloom. For the occasion, all the area around the Church of St. Frediano is adorned with flowers and plants and the memory of St. Zita is revived, with even greater intensity, by her fellow townsmen.

Outside the chapel there is a St. *Bartholomew* also attributed to Andrea della Robbia.The following Chapel of St. Biagio, also called the Cenami Chapel, contains a fine picture by the 17th century Pietro Paolini, portraying a *Deposition* and several wooden statues carved by Matteo Civitali. Out-side the chapel, there are a number of fragments of the altar of the Holy Sacrament, at which Civitali worked in 1489, but the altar was later dismantled and almost destroyed.

The last chapel on the right, the Micheli Chapel, houses an *Assumption* in carved and painted

One of the splendid frescoes in St. Augustine's Chapel, painted by the Bolognese artist Amico Aspertini at the beginning of the 16th century, depicting the legendary Transfer of the Holy Effigy from Luni to Lucca.

Trenta Chapel: altar frontal by Jacopo della Quercia (1422). In the centre, Madonna and Child.

wood by Masseo Civitali (Matteo's nephew), dating from the first few years of the 16th century. Making our way towards the main altar, we may admire the remains of a splendid cosmatesque floor dating from the 12th century. It was moved to this spot at the end of the 17th century when the altar was placed here; originally it was in the area occupied by the choir-stalls.

At the top of the left nave there is a monolith of limestone which probably came from the Roman amphitheatre, like the material used to build the columns in the central nave. Next to it stands the only panel that is left of St. Frediano's tomb, which was tak-

en to pieces a long time ago.

In the left nave, the Trenta Chapel houses another masterpiece of 15th century sculpture. It is an elaborate *altar frontal*, yet another work by Jacopo della Quercia, who carved it in 1422, using a single block of marble. It is a polyptych, carved in a distinctly Gothic style, made up of five panels in each of which there is a religious figure.

In the centre there is a Madonna and Child, and to the sides St. Ursula, St Lawrence, St Jerome and St. Richard. In the panels underneath, there are bas-reliefs of a Pietà with two mourning figures, and scenes depicting either the miracles or the martyrdom of the saints on the frontal above.

The Trenta Chapel also contains an urn of the 3rd century AD which holds the remains of the Irish Saint Richard, who died during a pilgrimage to Lucca in 722, tombstones for Lorenzo Trenta and his wife with bas-reliefs by Jacopo della Quercia (1416), a statue of St. *Peter* by Civitali and the *Conception of Mary* by Francia dated 1511.

In St. Augustine's Chapel, we can admire a series of frescoes which, according to the art historian Vasari, are one of the finest works of the painter Amico Aspertini. Painted in 1508-9, the frescoes depict *Episodes in the life of St. Frediano*, *St Augustine baptized by St. Ambrose*, *The Birth of Christ* and the famous *Transfer of the Holy Effigy from Luni to Lucca*. Each picture has been studied with great attention, and is rich in realistic details, including the depiction of the faces of well-known citizens and the artist himself.

There is another fresco by Amico Aspertini in the church, but unfortunately it is in a very poor state of preservation; situated on the right side of the main doorway, it depicts the *Madonna with four Saints and an Angel*. The fresco on the left of the doorway, the *Visitation*, is attributed to the "Master of the Lathrop Tondo".

THE SACRISTY

There are some truly beautiful religious ornaments and vestments kept in the sacristy of the church, including a copper reliquary of the Rhine School, which perhaps belonged to St. Richard, since it was found in his tomb, and the splendid brocade parament woven by Lucca craftsmen in the

16th century and used to cover the columns and walls of the central nave during solemn services. There is also a rare example of proto-Islamic art: a bronze falcon with an inscription in Arabic which was originally located at the top of the façade, where a copy has been put in its place today.

Bell tower of the Church of San Frediano

3) PALAZZO PFANNER

Palazzo Pfanner, formerly called Palazzo Controni, is a splendid palace built around 1667. The name of the architect who designed it is unknown, but we can see that in designing the façade he followed the late 16th century style, and not the taste of the second half of the 17th century that tended towards the Baroque, which we find in the interior, in the ample reception room and in the particularly splendid staircase, with columns and pillars which create a grandiose effect.

The interior naturally houses numerous works of art. The first floor, for example, was decorated in the first few years of the 18th century by Pietro Scorzini, who frescoed it with magnificent imaginary views which now form a charming background to the *Permanent Costume Exhibition* of the 17th, 18th and 19th centuries, which was set up recently thanks to private donations and to the purchase of costumes manufactured in Lucca by the Town Authorities.

The 18th century gardens are just as elaborate as the interior, and are attributed to Filippo Juvarra, who stayed in Lucca for a time to complete work on the Palazzo Pubblico and to design the gardens of various country houses. The gardens are arranged with clever stage-like effects; at the centre of the garden there is a large octagonal pool, while elegant statues representing the months of the year, the seasons and various divinities flank the large central avenue, embellished with hedges and luxuriant lemon trees.

Nearby, in Piazza San Salvatore, we can see what is left of the 12th century *Veglio Tower* and the *Church of St. Saviour*, dating from the end of the same century. Above the door on the right-hand side wall of the church, an elaborate lintel carved in the same period by the Pisan sculptor Biduino depicts St. *Nicholas's Miracle*. The upper part of the façade was rebuilt in the 19th century in Gothic style. Inside, there are works by Zacchia da Vezzano, a *Madonna and Saints* by Ardenti and a 15th century altar by Stagi.

Right: *one of the staircases inside the palace.*
Below: *view of the palace garden.*

Above: *bell tower of the Church of Our Lady Corteorlandini, which rises above the buildings around the church;* **next page:** *detail of the 12th century lunette above the side door;* **below:** *a view of the Church of Our Lady Corteorlandini.*

4) CHURCH OF OUR LADY CORTEORLANDINI

This church (Santa Maria Corteor-landini) is also known as *Santa Maria Nera*, because it houses a Madonna from Loreto (with a black ebany face), and is a repro-duction of the Holy House of Loreto. Its more usual name de-rives from the old name of this spot: Corte Rolandinga, or Rolandinga Court. The façade dates from the 17th century, and only the side walls and apses be-long to the original 12th century building.

Rebuilt completely inside in 1719, it is one of the few examples of Baroque architecture in Lucca. The vaults were decorated with frescoes and stuccowork by Pietro Scorzini.

Palazzo Orsetti: detail of one of the fine entrance-doors, designed by Nicolao Civitali. Right: The sumptuous 18th century rooms inside Palazzo Orsetti.

5) PALAZZO ORSETTI

Between the 16th and 17th centuries, in the area between the Church of St. Frediano and Palazzo Mansi, many grand town houses were built by the more wealthy families of Lucca. Among these was *Palazzo Orsetti*, which was built in the first half of the 16th century. Designed by Nicolao Civitali, the building, which has now become the Town Hall, has two entrances on two different streets, both with splendid carved wood doors. The pillars and arches in grey stone are decorated with elegant bas-reliefs representing trophies, sphinxes, dragons and grotesque figures.

Inside the building there are some fine 18th century rooms to be visited, like the *Red Room*, the *Green Room*, the *Hall of Mirrors* and the *Echo Room*, all sumptuously embellished with original tapestries and paintings. A famous portrait of the composer Giacomo Puccini can be seen here, painted by Luigi de Servi in 1902.

6) PALAZZO MANSI

Built between the end of the 16th and the beginning of the 17th centuries, *Palazzo Mansi*, situated opposite the Church of St. Peregrine's, is an interesting example of the architecture in Lucca of its time; it reflects the quiet life of the town, far from the turmoil and artistic ferment of Florence, for example. This is why the exterior of residences built in this period was very simple, modest, almost anonymous; there is a total absence of showy decorations, rusticated masonry or elaborately framed windows. The focus was rather on the interior of the buildings, on the gardens, courtyards, loggias and inside rooms which, as in Palazzo Mansi, were embellished with splendid works of art which can still be seen there. Today, Palazzo Mansi houses the *National Picture Gallery*.

National Picture Gallery

On the ground floor there is a spacious entrance-hall leading to a courtyard, and rooms used for public events. On the upper floor there is an apartment which still contains the magnificent furnishings of the 18th and 19th centuries, and elaborate tapestries from Brussels, designed by Justus Egmont (1665), depicting episodes from the life of Queen Zenobia and the Emperor Aurelian, which decorate the walls of some of the elegant reception rooms.

But the real attraction of the apartment is the *Bridal Chamber*, an incredible room sumptuously decorated with golden stuccowork, with precious and elaborately embroidered silk fabrics, mirrors in ornate frames and frescoes, and a kind of "triumphal arch" decorated with cupids, caryatids and gilt vegetation,

Palazzo Mansi - The sumptuously decorated Bridal Chamber (18th century). Below: Portrait of a Young Man, one of Pontormo's most famous paintings, circa 1525.

which leads into the splendid alcove with its canopied bed. It is one of the most complete examples of the ornate Baroque style in decoration of the period.

In the adjacent rooms, which have now become a Museum, most of the works of art on show belong to the collection donated by the Grand Duke Leopold II of Tuscany when Lucca was annexed to his territory in 1847.

Many of these works come from the Medici Wardrobe and date from the 16th and 17th centuries. Among the artists represented we will find: Tintoretto, Veronese, Guido Reni, Domenichino, the young Palma, Domenico Beccafumi and Pontormo.

Palazzo Mansi - National Picture Gallery - The Continence of Scipio (Domenico Beccafumi, 14th century).

7) CHURCH OF ST. PAOLINO

Dedicated to the first bishop of Lucca, this church is situated in the street of the same name and is the work of Baccio da Montelupo, who designed and built it in the period 1522-36.

It is the only example of a Renaissance church in Lucca and is distinguished by its elegant façade in white marble, with its simple decorative divisions. The lower level is united to the central level by two large scrolls which are repeated, in smaller dimensions, at a higher level.

The interior, in the form of a Latin cross, has a large central nave and two very small side naves, and houses precious paintings and wooden sculptures. The tribune is decorated with frescoes which narrate the story of the *Legend of St. Paolino*; the two lower ones are by Filippo Gherardi, a Lucca artist of the 17th century, and the two

above are by Stefano Cassiani, known as "il Certosino", and also date from the 17th century.

❧❀❦

8) PIAZZA SAN MICHELE

Piazza San Michele has been the real heart of Lucca ever since Roman times, when the area was occupied by the forum. As well as the monumental Church of St. Michael's, *Palazzo Pretorio* (*Magistrate's Hall*, formerly *Palazzo del Podestà*) also stands on the square. This building dates back to the end of the 15th century, and has a ground-floor portico and spacious mullioned windows. It was designed either by the architect Matteo Civitali or his son Nicolao in 1492; in 1589 another Civitali, Vincenzo this time, was commissioned to double the depth of the loggia.

Another interesting building standing in the square is *Palazzo del Decanato*, which is connected to the church by a kind of bridge. De-

Interior of the Church of St. Paolino.

signed by the architect Francesco Marti, it dates from the 16th century and was built over a previous building, *Palazzo degli Anziani* (*the Elders' Hall*).

The rest of the large square is occupied by 13th and 14th century houses built in the Romanesque and Gothic styles. The house where the composer, Giacomo Puccini, was born is situated in Via di Poggio, opposite the church; today the house contains the Puccini Foundation and Museum.

Palazzo Pretorio, in Piazza San Michele.

THE CITY OF MUSIC

From as far back as the Middle Ages, Lucca has developed a prestigious musical tradition which enjoyed a period of particular celebrity in the 16th century, when the brothers **Gioseffo** and **Francesco Guami** were born there, considered two of the greatest European composers of the time by the critics. And they only marked the beginning of what was to be a long series of musicians from Lucca, who would be considered among the greatest composers of their times.

The first of this series is **Luigi Boccherini**, who lived in the second half of the 18th century and composed famous minuets. Born into a family of musicians, he toured half the courts of Europe, especially those of Madrid and Berlin at the time of Frederick II of Prussia. His compositions range from chamber music, in which he is considered a key figure, to overtures, from divertissements to pieces of sacred music. He also wrote an opera, "La Clementina".

In the second half of the 19th century, **Alfredo Catalani** began his career as a composer in Lucca before moving to Paris and then to Milan to continue his studies; in Milan, he was to play no small part in the Scapigliatura movement.

He was a pianist of exceptional sensitivity and he composed several works, including "La Falce", "Elda" (1880), "Dejanice" (1883), "Loreley" (1890) and "Wally" (1892).

It was in Lucca that one of the most famous composers of the late 19th century was born, **Giacomo Puccini**, who was born in 1858 in Via di Poggio, in the house which now contains the Puccini Museum. Puccini belonged to a dynasty of composers who came from the valley of the Serchio; he began to study music in Lucca and then completed his studies at the Conservatory in Milan, where he studied with Amilcare Ponchielli. He wrote some of the finest works of the beginning of this century. We should mention "Manon Lescaut", with which his fame spread beyond his home country and which was first performed at the Royal Theatre in Turin in 1893. It was followed in 1896 by "La Bohème", perhaps his best-known opera, "Madama Butterfly" in 1904, "La Fanciulla del West" which was performed in New York in 1910,

and the famous trilogy of one-act operas designed to be performed together, "Il Tabarro", "Suor Angelica" and "Gianni Schicchi". His last opera was "Turandot", which he left unfinished and which was completed from his notes by Franco Alfano.

Puccini composed almost all his operas in Tuscany, at his home at Torre del Lago, which is now called Torre del Lago Puccini, a village situated on the banks of the picturesque Lake of Massaciuccoli. The house is open to visitors; it still contains much of the original furniture and many mementoes of the famous composer who lived there.

9) CHURCH OF ST. MICHAEL IN THE FORUM

This elaborate church, designed following the style used in Lucca and Pisa in the 12th century, was built in several stages, and was only completed in the 14th century. The first records we have of a church of St. Michael in the Forum date back to the 8th century but there are few remains of this early building.

THE FAÇADE

The various periods in which the church was built can be easily traced in the present building; in the towering façade, for example, the lower half is clearly Romanesque while the upper half is influenced by the Gothic style which we have already noted in St. Martin's Cathedral. The similarity with the Cathedral is evident in the rows of arches, in the small, elaborately carved columns of green and white marble, and in the delicate inlaid work which occupies all the space above the arches.

At the top of the façade there is an enormous Romanesque statue of St. Michael the Archangel, depicted in his victory over the dragon; by his side there are two angels blowing horns, standing on tabernacles, dating from a later period. On the right-hand corner of the façade there is a fine *Madonna and Child* by Matteo Civitali. During restoration work in the last century, new sculptures were added to the façade; if we look carefully between the arches, we can see the heads of famous personalities such as Garibaldi, Victor Emmanuel II, Cavour and many others. At the same time, many of the original columns were replaced and are now in the Museum at Villa Guinigi. The lower part of the façade is

formed by a series of blind arches which continue along the side walls.

The bell tower, built over the transept, is divided into several levels with rows of arches; it belongs to the first stage of construction of the church, whereas the very top of the tower was rebuilt in the last century.

INTERIOR

The interior is pure Romanesque; it consists of three naves separat-

ed by columns, a transept and a semicircular apse. The original triangular beam structure of the ceiling was replaced by a vaulted ceiling in the 16th century.

The church is full of splendid works of art. Beginning from the first altar on the right, we can see a beautiful *Madonna and Child* in glazed terracotta by Andrea della Robbia. Further up on the right, there is a fine painting by Pietro Paolini, the *Martyrdom of St. Andrew*. A 13th century crucifix painted on a wooden panel, with the figure of Christ in light relief, can be seen in the right transept, while in the left transept there is a fine painting by Filippino Lippi depicting St. *Sebastian*, St *Jerome*, St *Rocco and* St. *Helen*. Nearby there is a fragment of a lost tomb carved by Raffaello da Montelupo in 1522, depicting a *Madonna and Child* in high relief.

The remains of the 8th century church can be seen near the presbytery.

10) CHURCH OF ST. ALEXANDER

St. Alexander's Church is one of the few examples in Lucca of Romanesque architecture which has not been radically altered in the course of time. In fact its original structure is still intact, making it into the oldest church to have been preserved in the town.

Dating from the 11th century, it is a perfect example of the town's Romanesque architecture, which distinguished itself from Lombard and Pisan architecture of the same period.

The lower part of the simple marble façade is bare, undecorated, its uniform white surface interrupted only by grey horizontal strips and a classical doorway. On the upper part of the façade the only concession to decoration is a simple statue of a seated St. Alexander, above which there is a plain mullioned window.

The interior is designed in the form of a basilica, with three naves, and is as simple and basic as the exterior. The central nave is separated from the side naves by columns with splendid capitals and by pillars which originally marked the area of the choir-stalls. Above the columns, two ledges run along the length of the nave, in the same simple style. As in the case of many churches in Lucca, some of the columns and capitals come from buildings dating from Roman times.

Simple Romanesque façade of the Church of St.Alexander (11th century).

11) PIAZZA NAPOLEONE

The name of the square reminds us of the period in which it was designed. It was opened, in fact, in 1806, at the wish of the princess Elisa Baciocchi Bonaparte.

In order to make room for this square, a whole block of the town was demolished, including a church as well as other buildings. Many projects were prepared and a series of ideas and proposals put forward, which were only partly implemented.

The square is of vast dimensions, shaded by enormous plane-trees. In the centre there is a *Monument to Maria Luigi di Borbone*, one of the women who governed Lucca, by Lorenzo Nottolini (1843).

❦

12) PALAZZO DUCALE

Also called the *Palazzo Pubblico* (*Public Palace*) or *Palazzo della Signoria* (*Lord's Palace*), the *Palazzo Ducale* (*Ducal Palace*) stands on the spot previously occupied by the *Augusta Fortress*, which Castruccio Castracani, of the Antelminelli family, had built in 1322, on plans by Giotto. On the death of Castruccio, the Pisans occupied the fortress and later the people of Lucca destroyed it in a fit of mob violence because it had become a symbol of Pisan oppression.

Only the noble residence which had been part of the fortress was saved; it was first used as a residence by the Elders of the Republic, then by Paolo Guinigi when he was Lord of Lucca at the beginning of the 15th century, when he had it enlarged. It later returned to the Elders and since then it has remained the adminis-

trative and political centre of the town.

In 1578 Bartolomeo Ammannati was entrusted with rebuilding the palace. Part of his work is still visible, including the beautiful gallery overlooking the *Cortile degli Svizzeri*, or Courtyard of the Swiss Guards, and the portico underneath it, which once formed the façade of the palace. All the left side of the present façade is his work too. His plans, however, were not completed because of financial problems and it was only in 1728 that work continued on the side of the building with the monumental entrance, and Filippo Juvarra was commissioned to design the second courtyard, after part of Ammannati's work was demolished because it was unstable and dangerous.

During the Napoleonic period, Elisa Baciocchi Bonaparte had the large square created on the eastern side of the building (which then became the main façade); her intention was to have military parades in the square, and thus confer on the town the air of a European capital. She gave the square its name of Piazza Napoleone, after her brother. The square was designed by the architects Lazzarini and Bienaimé.

In the first half of the 19th century, the Bourbon Maria Luisa appointed Lorenzo Nottolini Royal Architect, and then entrusted him with numerous rebuilding and extension plans, including the majestic staircase leading into the palace from the Courtyard of the Swiss Guards and a passageway between the two courtyards, known as Carriage Passage.

It was the interior of the palace in particular which Maria Luisa wished to alter. She commissioned the Gallery of Statues and she also re-arranged the rooms of the "piano nobile" to form three apartments: the Queen's reception rooms, the King's reception rooms and the State apartments, which included conference rooms and the Sovereign's Cabinet. Unfortunately the splendid furniture in these apartments became State property, together with the palace itself, when Lucca was annexed to the Kingdom of Italy and it was distributed to the various royal palaces scattered around Italy.

Today the visitor can see the Royal Staircase, the Gallery of Statues, the Loggia and some of the State rooms, such as the Swiss Chamber.

Piazza Napoleone, situated in the centre of Lucca, with Palazzo Ducale, the former ducal palace which now houses administrative offices.

13) CHURCH OF ST. ROMANO

Just behind the Palazzo Ducale we find Piazza San Romano, where the church of the same name is situated. Consecrated in 1281, it was built on the remains of an early oratory. We can still see part of the original church, in the side with arches forming burial recesses in the Gothic style.

The church was enlarged at the end of the following century (1373); it was made higher, the apse was rebuilt in brick and five side chapels were added. The bricks used were taken from the nearby Augusta Fortress, which had been demolished.

The present interior, in the form of a Latin cross with a single nave and large arched windows, is Baroque, dating from 1661. Once full of works of art, the church still houses the tomb of St. Romano behind the main altar, carved by Matteo Civitali in the 15th century.

Outside the church, there are several tombstones piled up together which used to be part of the church floor; dating from the 14th and 15th centuries, they await a final location. Among them is the tombstone of Capoana Donoratico, wife of the famous Ugolino della Gherardesca mentioned by Dante in his "Divine Comedy", and the tombs of the seven Constables of the Augusta Fortress, knights of Teutonic origin.

In the underground basement of the church it is possible to follow an archaeological route showing the different stages of its construction, from the early Christian period to the High Middle Ages.

Church of St. Romano.

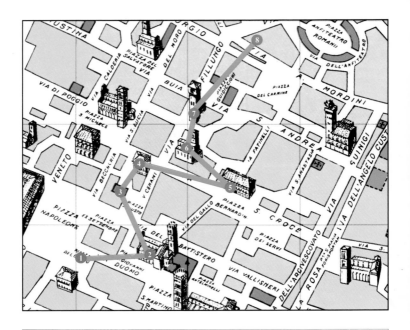

1) PIAZZA DEL GIGLIO

The *Teatro del Giglio* ("Lily" *Theatre*), with its elegant neoclassical façade, is situated in this square. Designed by the architect Lazzarini, the theatre was famous at the beginning of the last century for being the first theatre to show new plays, competing with the San Carlo Theatre in Naples and La Scala in Milan.

Two other attractive mansions face onto the square, *Palazzo Arnolfini* and *Palazzo Paoli*, and in the centre there is a monument to Giuseppe Garibaldi.

2) CHURCH OF ST. JOHN AND REPARATA

This church was the Cathedral of Lucca before the privilege passed to St. Martin's. The original church dates back to the 5th or 6th century, as recent excavations have shown, but the church which stands today dates from the 12th century. The façade was rebuilt in 1595, but has preserved its ornate Romanesque doorway, with its splendid lintel carved with bas-reliefs of Lombard inspiration.

The Romanesque interior is in the form of a Latin cross, divided into three naves and a transept. The columns used to separate the naves are of varying size, with different shafts and capitals, probably because they come from several buildings demolished in the period of Imperial Rome. From the left arm of the transept one can enter the baptistry, added to the church in the 14th century, which is square in shape and covered by a large pointed dome. The original baptismal font, dating from the early Middle Ages, can be seen in the centre of the baptistry, as well as some fragments of a black and white Roman floor, which are approximately three metres beneath the present floor level.

3) CHURCH OF ST. GIUSTO

The Romanesque *Church of St. Giusto* dates back to the end of the 12th century, with a handsome marble façade in which there are three fine doorways with the high, raised lunettes typical of churches in Lucca.

The central doorway has a splendidly carved lintel, and the central lunette is decorated with a painting of a Madonna and Child and is framed by bas-reliefs.

The interior, divided into three naves, has unusual terracotta pillars. Restored in 1661-62, it is decorated with elaborate stuccowork.

The doorway of the Church of St. John and Reparata.

Detail of the lunette above the central doorway of the Church of St. Giusto.

4) PALAZZO CENAMI

Further on, at the corner of Canto d'Arco, the old name for Via Santa Croce, we come across the imposing *Palazzo Cenami*, formerly called Palazzo Arnolfini, built around 1530 by Nicolao Civitali, who was inspired by some of the complex stylistic features of the Florentines. It is an exceptional building for the way it was incorporated into a medieval setting.

We should notice several architectural features which were unusual for a building of its time in Lucca - for example, the rusticated masonry in a sunburst pattern around both the high windows of the two central floors and the street-level cellar windows, and the sturdy stone base which runs around the whole of the outside walls of the mansion, highlighted by a thick ledge under which there are numerous stone benches for passers-by to sit on.

The interior opens onto a large rectangular courtyard surrounded by an elegant loggia.

5) PALAZZO BERNARDINI

At the end of Via del Gallo there is a square which takes its name from the building which dominates it: *Palazzo Bernardini*, which belonged to Martino Bernardini, who had a residence built outside the walls similar to it, called the Villa delle Quattro Torri (Villa of the Four Towers).

The town house was designed by Nicolao Civitali, though the central part of it is older, dating from the early 16th century (1517-23).

One of its most characteristic features was the large, mullioned windows on the central floor, which have since been replaced, and another was its street-level stone benches which still exist today.

It is one of the most important 16th century buildings in Lucca, because of its considerable size and its stylistic features inspired by Florentine mannerism. The location of the mansion on what was one of the main streets of the old town is the proof of how important it was for the distinguished families of the town to build their residences in strategic positions.

In the 18th century the square in front of the mansion was created and work was carried out to widen it in both directions. The entrance to the mansion with its rusticated double-arched doorway is of great elegance; the wrought iron design above the door which we can still see today is original.

THE REBELLIOUS STONE

There is a popular legend regarding a stone in the jamb of the first window on the right of the main door of Palazzo Bernardini; it is called the "miracle stone" or "devil's stone", because it is oddly curved, as if it were made of wood.

According to popular explanations, the curvature is due to the refusal of the stone to return to its original position, flat against the wall, because originally there was a sacred picture in its place, which was removed and destroyed during restoration works.

Palazzo Bernardini.

6) CHURCH OF ST. CHRISTOPHER

The handsome façade in white and grey marble of St. *Christopher's Church* is found in a recess along Via Fillungo. The church dates back to the 12th century; the first records of it are dated 1053 but it was only completed in the following century. The upper part of the façade, with the large rose-window and rows of small blind arches, belongs to the end of the 14th century.

The Romanesque interior is divided into three naves separated by rectangular pillars and by four columns which support a large arch near the presbytery. There is a fine 14th century fresco of the Virgin; underneath, a tablet commemorates two of Matteo Civitali's sons, who died while still young. The artist himself is buried in the church.

The strange iron bars on the façade once served to measure the combs, grips and other parts of the textile looms of the town; it was here in fact that the Corporation of Merchants was based, and it was the Corporations' officials who decided to place the bars outside the church.

In front of the church is the so-called Torre del Travaglio (Tower of Suffering) and the medieval house where Matteo Civitali lived. The building is also known as Monna Vanna's house and was restored in 1925, when the town authorities began to carry out work in the town to restore its medieval appearance, after the Bourbon Duke Carlo Ludovico had ordered most of the buildings in Lucca to be plastered over around the middle of the last century.

7) TOWER OF THE HOURS

Towering above Via Fillungo is one of the town's landmarks: the 12th century *Tower of The Hours*, which has probably been preserved up to now thanks to its public clock, installed in 1471. In fact, of the numerous towers which once existed, only the Guinigi Tower and the Tower of the Hours still remain today.

Every noble family had a tower built as part of their residence; according to records, there were at least 130, and probably there were more. Unfortunately, the fate of the towers often followed that of their owners; if the owners were ruined or banished, the towers of their houses were often demolished or made lower, and in the time of Castruccio Castracani, the building materials from demolished towers were used to build the Augusta Fortress.

For a period the Tower was also called the *Tower of Contention* because it was the object of contention among rival families, each of whom claimed it as theirs.

Near the Tower, there is a typically narrow medieval street - *Chiasso Barletti* - with a row of houses which belonged to the Barletti family in the 13th century and which are one of the best examples still remaining of medieval tower-houses.

8) PALAZZO TRENTA

The oldest mansion in Lucca to have kept its original structure is *Palazzo Trenta*, which dates back to the first half of the 15th century.

The mansion was built with very different construction criteria from those used before. It does not contain a ground-floor portico, for

Above: *detail of the decoration of the central doorway of the Church of* St. Christopher.
Below: *the medieval Tower of the Hours.*

example, which we find in many buildings in the town with the aim of creating more pavement space; in Palazzo Trenta, the façade is full and even, apart from the string-course ledge which runs underneath the first floor windows. The windows are also a new feature: high and large, they draw attention to the size of the façade. The mansion stands on the edge of Via Fillungo, adapting to the street's irregular course so closely that at one point it even forms a wide, almost imperceptible corner.

Not far away is St. Augustine's Church; dating from the 14th century, its bell tower was built over the arches of the old Roman theatre, of which a few remains are still visible in several houses in Via S. Sebastiano and in Piazza delle Grazie.

VIA FILLUNGO: THE HEART OF LUCCA

Via Fillungo, the long street which stretches across a large part of the centre of Lucca, was named after the Castle of Fillungo, in the Garfagnana hills, which belonged to the Falabrina family who also owned several buildings in this street.

Today, the life of the town centres on Via Fillungo; for the people of Lucca it is a favourite place for a stroll and is full of shops.

It winds its lengthy way uninterruptedly, bending occasionally and becoming narrower in some places, wider in others.

Via Fillungo has been defined as a "long, fluctuating ribbon" on which buildings have been continually added and altered over the centuries, since the 1200s. Fortunately the additions and alterations have always blended in harmony with each other. The street is very narrow and the proximity of the buildings opposite to each other create a cosy atmosphere; in some spots, one almost has the impression of being indoors.

For the people of Lucca the shops situated along the street are more than a place to make their purchases; they are also a place to meet their friends and acquaintances, to stroll, to pass a free hour or so. The shops have always been an integral part of the architectural structure of the street and it would be true to say that Via Fillungo would not be the same without them.

The cafés along the street have also contributed to making the street of such importance for the history of the town and even, perhaps, for the history of Italian literature in the first half of this century. The famous 19th century Caffè Di Simo, situated halfway along the street, was a meeting-place in the 1940s for writers such as Giuseppe Ungaretti, Giuseppe De Robertis, Enrico Pea and Guglielmo Petroni, whose literary evenings left their mark in the history of Italian 20th century literature.

A walk along Via Fillungo is without doubt an excellent way of becoming acquainted with the history of Lucca, with its active public and private life. Many of the town houses belonging to important families are located here, witnesses to the alternating fortunes of their owners; many of the town's churches are also to be found here, still full of the proof of the devotion of its inhabitants; here too are most of the town's shops, of great importance for a town of textile manufacturers and tradespeople. If there is a street in Lucca which can tell the story of the town, that street can only be Via Fillungo.

Via Fillungo.

The custom of building *villas*, or country houses, in the area around Lucca dates back six centuries and has become one of the distinguishing features of its hills and countryside. Initially, the villas began as country residences built by the flourishing merchant class, which was more interested in the agricultural produce of its property than in making a show of its wealth.

The enormous number of these villas - almost six hundred - and their complexity make this historical and architectural heritage into a cultural phenomenon worthy of study.

The period in which the phenomenon reached its climax was the 16th century, and we will find many of the villas date from then. Their distinguishing features were: their solid, square form, in some cases with wings standing forward from the central part of the house, their elaborate gardens, a loggia at the back of the house and inside, on the "piano nobile", a central salon from which doors led to other rooms.

ROYAL VILLA OF MARLIA

The origins of this villa are very old; initially the residence of the Duke of Tuscia, it passed into the hands of the Avvocati family and later became the property of the extremely wealthy Buonvisi family; when they went bankrupt in 1651, the villa passed to the Orsetti family. The Orsettis rebuilt the villa and had superb gardens laid. Little is left of the work commissioned by the Orsettis but from the drawings left to

Royal Villa of Marlia.

us, we can see that the style was typically Renaissance.

In 1811, Elisa Baciocchi, princess of Lucca, insisted on having the villa from the Orsetti family. She wanted to transform it into a royal residence, and the work she had done radically altered the villa. Its appearance changed completely, although its size remained the same. The rusticated masonry was replaced by smooth, even surfaces; at the back of the villa, a portico was added with a terrace on top of it; inside, the arrangement of rooms underwent a metamorphosis with the creation of vast new salons, decorated and furnished in strict neoclassical style. The entrance was made majestic by the presence of the two buildings in pure Napoleonic style which opened onto a spacious, semicircular courtyard, embellished with hedges and marble vases.

In order to facilitate travel between her two royal residences, the one in town and the one outside the walls, Elisa Baciocchi had a gate opened in the town walls, Porta Elisa, through which a perfectly straight road was built to lead directly to the country villa which was called "royal" from then onwards.

The original architectural layout of the 17th century garden was not altered but the garden itself was extended enormously and re-arranged in the "English style", as fashion dictated at that time. The pool and play of water at the back of the villa was preserved, together with the sequence of the lemon garden, the access to the fountain, the Baroque "greenery" theatre and the *Palazzina dell'Orologio*, or *Clock House*.

The estate was extended enormously, incorporating the "Bishop's Villa", which had its own big gardens; this lengthened the view from the front of the Villa considerably, doubling the space there, which was then landscaped into a long, wide lawn surrounded by trees and bushes, sloping gently towards a small lake.

The complex of buildings and gardens are well preserved; the park has recently been opened to visitors and for an important series of musical events which take place in the "greenery" theatre, where Nicolò Paganini often used to perform in the last century, when he was a frequent guest of the Baciocchis.

VILLA MANSI

Located at Segromigno, *Villa Mansi* is perhaps the most famous of Lucca's country houses. The most significant work on the Villa, which was first built in the second half of the 16th century, was carried out by the architect Muzio Oddi, who enlarged and transformed the façade in 1635.

Subsequent alterations on the Villa were carried out by the Abbot Gian Francesco Giusti, who modified the façade, embellishing the upper part with balustrades decorated with statues, and later by Juvarra, in the second quarter of the 18th century, who was entrusted with landscaping the gardens. He created a masterly play of scenic effects, alternating wide views with intersecting prospects; at the same time, he replaced brusque drops in the level of the ground with gentle slopes, channelled water harmoniously along routes studied for their artistic effect, and created new gardens enclosed

Elegant façade of **Villa Mansi** *at* **Segromigno.**

by elegantly-shaped hedges.

Further alterations in the 19th century almost completely cancelled the Sicilian architect's work, creating a garden with a more natural appearance in accordance with the fashion of the time.

Inside the Villa, there are numerous works of art: frescoes on mythological subjects by Tofanelli, paintings by Pompeo Batoni and Longhi, several landscapes by Salvator Rosa and a collection of bronzes from the 16th and 17th centuries. The furnishings reflect the neoclassical taste which was in fashion in the Napoleonic period.

VILLA TORRIGIANI

The spectacular *Villa Torrigiani* at Camigliano was first built in the 16th century, but was altered several times in the 17th and early 18th centuries, probably following plans by the architect Muzio Oddi.

The Villa brings out the relationship between architecture and nature more than any other of the country houses in the area, thanks to a magnificent avenue lined with cypresses, 700 metres long, which leads up to the entrance, and which affords a splendid view of the house framed between the rows of cypresses.

The ornate façade is richly decorated with statues, niches, recesses and balconies, and is enlivened by attractive colour contrasts created by the different materials which were used to make it: sandstone, tufa, grey stone and marble. It is unique among the country houses in this area, which usually follow 16th century architectural styles closely; the only feature it has kept from this period is the loggia at the back.

Inside the house there are two unusual staircases of elliptical shape, which are illuminated from above to great effect.

The furnishings and decor inside the house are Baroque; there are frescoes and paintings by Pietro Scorzini and Vincenzo Dandini, who painted the wall panels in the central salon with *The Battle of the Amazons against the Romans, Aurelian triumphing with Queen Zenobia* and, on the ceiling, *The Apotheosis of Aurelian.*

The gardens are without doubt one of the most important and masterly examples of 17th century landscape gardening in the Lucca area. They are laid out on different levels, with the separate areas as clearly defined and limited as if they were indoor rooms. The level of the flower garden, divided with precision into flowerbeds, begins at the nymphaeum, which is embellished with a play of water considered extremely elaborate for the time, and slopes gradually down to the wall at the bottom, where flights of steps lead to the level of the fish-pool. The whole scene is enhanced by pools of different shapes and a circular fountain at the back of the house.

Villa Torrigiani.

THE CASTLES OF NOZZANO, MONTECARLO AND ALTOPASCIO

Of all the fortifications erected by Lucca in the past to defend its territorial borders towards Pisa and Florence, only the castles of Nozzano and Montecarlo still remain today.

Nozzano is a fort guarding the right bank of the River Serchio, built on calcareous rock rising up from the plain in front of the powerful castle of Ripafratta, which belonged to Pisa.

Its many-towered castle, dating from the 14th century, was built on the hill overlooking the village of Nozzano. One of the towers of the old castle has been transformed into the bell tower of the church.

Montecarlo is a fortified village on the top of a hill, and is the centre for the production of the famous Bianco, an excellent local white wine. The fort has been preserved intact, consisting in an ancient tower, a 14th century central part and a later extension built by the Medicis in the 16th century, after the village passed into the hands of the Florentines.

The village has kept ist medieval walls, gates and stone-paved streets, onto which old shop open their doors. There is also a tiny 18th century theatre which alone makes a visit to the village worthwhile, and a marvellous view over the vineyards, olive groves and woods of the Nievole Valley.

The castle and fortified village of *Altopascio* deserves special mention for its bell tower, which is one of the most imposing and stylistically perfect bell towers in the whole of the Tuscan countryside. It was visible from a great distance and used to be an essential landmark for travellers who had lost their way to the village. One can still hear the tolling of the "Smarrita" ("Lost Way"), the bell which used to ring for an hour after sunset to help pilgrims reach the village safe and sound, if darkness overtook them in the nearby marshes or woods.

The castle dates back to the year 1000, and was built to provide a certain degree of safety for the important European road, called the "Francigena - Romea Way", which connected the north of Europe to the centre of Christianity from the time of Emperor Charlemagne. Altopascio was a stopping-place for pilgrims, offering them protection and even medical treatment if necessary in a fortifed hospital which the Tau monastic order of knights had set up for this purpose.

BORGO A MOZZANO

On the road leading to the Garfagnana hills, there is an attractive village called *Borgo a Mozzano*. In the parish church of *St James (San Jacopo)*, we can admire several fine wooden sculptures, including a tabernacle from the late 16th century and a statue by Matteo Civitali. There are also several statues of the Robbia School in coloured terracotta. The nearby *Oratory of the Crucifix* houses a wooden crucifix from the 16th century and some terracotta statues of the same century.

Just outside the village is an un-

Mary Magdalene's Bridge.

usual, hump-backed bridge across the river Serchio, called *Mary Magdalene's Bridge* or the *Devil's Bridge*. It spans the river on its four asymmetrical arches and is of great visual effect; begun at the wish of Countess Matilde of Canossa in the 11th century, it was completed in the 14th century.

❧❀❧

BAGNI DI LUCCA

Bagni di Lucca is a well-known spa town situated at the foot of the Hill of Corsena, and incorporates a series of hamlets along the banks of the River Lima.

One of these hamlets is Ponte a Serraglio, which developed around the bridge built by Castruccio Castracani in 1317, and in the immediate vicinity we find Bagni Caldi ("Hot Baths"), where the main spa establishments and baths are located, in which the temperature of the sulphureous and radioactive water ranges between 39°C and 54°C.

The waters were already well known in the 11th century, and reached the height of their fame during the last century. The town was frequented by nobles from Lucca and by a large number of writers, poets and artists, the most famous being Montaigne, Lord Byron, Heine, Carducci and D'Azeglio, who have left a record of their enjoyable visits to this pleasant resort in their writings.

Many tourists still visit the resort, especially the British, who have built an Anglican church and a cemetery here.

BARGA

Barga is an important town in the part of the Serchio valley which lies in the Garfagnana hills. Handed to the Rolandinghi (or Rolandini) family of Lucca as a feud in the 10th century, it was granted certain privileges by Matilde of Canossa in 1090, which were reinstated by Frederick Barbarossa. After being fought over by Lucca, Pisa and Florence, towards the middle of the 14th century it submitted to Florence, to which it linked its destiny until 1847.

One enters the town through the fine *Porta Reale* (*Royal Gate*), decorated with a Della Robbia terracotta of the *Madonna and Child with Angels*.

The *Cathedral* is in Piazzale dell'Arringo; like most Tuscan churches it has been rebuilt and altered many times, in this case in the 9th and 14th centuries. The side chapels were built later. In the course of time it has been turned around to face the other way; what is now the façade used to be the back of the church.

The façade still contains Romanesque elements and is embellished with a double row of small decorated arches. Over the side door there is an interesting carved lintel attributed to Biduino (12th century), depicting a banquet scene. A fine crenellated bell tower stands at one side.

The interior is divided into three naves by pillars; the central nave contains a handsome 12th century pulpit, carved with bas-reliefs including an *Annunciation* and a *Nativity*. It stands on four red marble columns; the front columns rest on lions, while the back columns rest on the shoulders of a bearded old man.

Around the presbytery there are fine marble parapets dating from the 13th century and in the apse there is a beautiful wooden statue of *St Christopher*. The Chapel of the Sacrament is decorated with beautiful Della Robbia terracottas. The church is also embellished with 14th century frescoes and sculptures by Bigarelli's school.

Back outside, the *Palazzo Pretorio*, or *Magistrate's Hall*, stands on the left of the Cathedral; the small 14th century loggia houses the *Prehistoric Museum of the Garfagnana*, with its burial objects and stone age fossils found in the area.

Just outside the village is the 16th century *Church of St Francis* (*San Francesco*), which one enters through the cloister, and which contains several altars by Della Robbia.

***

COREGLIA ANTELMINELLI

In another interesting village, *Coreglia Antelminelli*, situated in the Garfagnana hills, we can visit the lovely *Church of St Michael* (*San Michele*). Of 13th century origins, it was altered several times in the course of time; there is a fine *St Michael* on the façade attributed to Matteo Civitali and, inside, a beautiful *Annunciation* from the 14th century.

In the village we may also visit the 9th century *Church of St Martin* (*San Martino*), the *Town Hall* with its typical Renaissance façade, and *Palazzo Rossi*, which houses an ethnological exhibition.

***

CASTELVECCHIO PASCOLI

This is the village in which the poet Giovanni Pascoli spent the last days of his life. The house where he lived is on a hill just before the village; it was for him a place of refuge and quiet and a source of inspiration for many of his works, in particular a collection of poems which he named "I Canti di Castelvecchio" as well for as most of his other works.

The mortal remains of the poet are kept in the chapel in his house, together with those of his sister Maria.

TORRE DEL LAGO PUCCINI

Anyone who wishes to see the places which inspired so many of Giacomo Puccini's operas must visit the Lake of Massaciuccoli, and the modern town of Torre del Lago which stands on its banks. Situated at the foot of the far end of the Apuan Alps, not far from Lucca, the lake is where Puccini often chose to retire to compose his operas.

It is possible to visit the composer's house, where the furnishings, objects and souvenirs which Puccini enjoyed to have around him are still kept.

One of the rooms in the house has been transformed into a chapel in which the composer's mortal remains are kept.

Torre del Lago Puccini - Lake of Massaciuccoli.

Giacomo **Puccini.**

VIAREGGIO

The main seaside resort of the Versilian coast, *Viareggio*, is well known for its beaches, its shady pinewoods, its harbour and its famous Carnival. In 1170 it was a *castrum*, or fortress, belonging to Lucca; it had an important harbour and was provided with an imposing tower which guarded the Via Regia (Royal Way), from which the town acquired its name. It developed and expanded between the 18th and 19th centuries, under Bourbon rule, especially under Maria Luisa. The building of its elegant hotels and numerous beach establishments began at the beginning of this century. The former Town Hall, now called *Palazzo delle Muse*, houses an Archaeological Museum, *Museo Archeologico* C.A. *Blanc*, in which a varied range of objects are exhibited, the result of archaeological excavations in the area. Of particular interest are the finds from an Etruscan village of pile-dwellings which existed between the 8th and 3rd centuries BC, among which we can see a number of wooden statues, and objects made out of pottery and bronze, found in San Rocchino di Campo Casali. The Museum also houses many other finds from the Stone and Copper Ages, as well as objects found in tombs discovered in the caves of Pian Mommio, which had been buried along with the dead for use in the after-life.

Viareggio - The harbour.

USEFUL INFORMATION

LUCCA TOURIST BOARD
Piazza Guidiccioni 2
Tel. 0583 / 491205

TOURIST OFFICE - LUCCA TOWN COUNCIL
Vecchia Porta S. Donato P.le Verdi
Tel. 0583 / 442935 - 36

TOURIST OFFICE - LUCCA PROVINCE OFFICES
Cortile degli Svizzeri
Tel. 0583 / 4171

PUBLIC TRANSPORT

LUCCA BUS & COACH STATIONS
C.L.A.P. - P.le Verdi   Tel. 0583 / 587897
Lazzi - P.le Verdi   Tel. 0583 / 584876

LUCCA RAILWAY STATION
Piazza Ricasoli   Tel. 0583 / 47013

BICYCLE HIRE SERVICE
Casermetta San Donato (near the town walls)   Tel. 0583 / 442935

TAXIS
Piazza Napoleone Tel. 0583 / 492691
Piazza Stazione   Tel. 0583 / 494989
P.le Verdi   Tel. 0583 / 581305
Piazza S.Maria   Tel. 0583 / 494190
Campo di Marte (Hospital)
Tel. 0583 / 950623

LUCCA AIRPORT (E. SQUAGLIA)
Tassignano (Capannori)Tel. 0583 / 936062
(domestic tourist and commercial traffic -
executive airplane and helicopter traffic -
airtaxi service - air rescue base)

PUBLIC SERVICES AND FACILITIES

POST OFFICE
Via Vallisneri 2   Tel. 0583 / 46669

PUBLIC TELEPHONE CENTRE
Via Cenami 19   Opening hours 7 / 23

POLICE STATION
Via Cavour 38   Tel. 0583 / 4551

CARABINIERI POLICE STATION
Cortile degli Svizzeri 4   Tel. 0583 / 47821

MUNICIPAL POLICE
Via S. Giustina 32   Tel. 0583 / 442727

A.C.I. ITALIAN AUTOMOBILE CLUB
Via Catalani 59   Tel. 0583 / 582 626

TRAFFIC POLICE
Via Pisana 352   Tel. 0583 / 312555

LOST PROPERTY OFFICE
c /o Lucca Town Hall (Comune)
Ufficio Economato - Via C. Battisti 10
Tel. 0583 / 442388

LUCCA HOSPITAL
Via dell' Ospedale   Tel. 0583 / 9701

MUSEUMS AND TOURIST SIGHTS

CATHEDRAL MUSEUM
Piazza del Duomo   Tel. 0583 / 490530
Closed on Mondays - Opening hours:
Nov/ Apr 10/13 - 15/18; May/ Oct
9.30/18; Groups: booking obligatory.

RISORGIMENTO MUSEUM
Cortile degli Svizzeri 6
Tel. 0583 / 91636
Visits must be booked 2 days in advance

NATIONAL MUSEUM AT VILLA GUINIGI
Via della Quarquonia
Tel. 0583 / 496033
Opening hours: Tue-Sun   9/14 -
Closed on Mondays, Christmas Day,
New Year's Day, 1 May.

PALAZZO MANSI NATIONAL PICTURE GALLERY AND MUSEUM
Via Galli Tassi   Tel. 0583 / 55570
Opening hours: working days 9/19 -
Sundays/holidays 9/14 - Closed on
Mondays, Christmas Day, New Year's
Day, 1 May.

GUINIGI TOWER
Via Sant' Andrea (Palazzo Guinigi)
Tel. 0583 / 48524
Opening hours: Nov - Feb 10/16.30; Mar -
Sep 9/19.30; Oct 10/18.

GIACOMO PUCCINI'S BIRTHPLACE AND THE PUCCINI FOUNDATION
Corte S. Lorenzo 9 (Via di Poggio)
Tel. 0583 / 584028
Closed on Mondays - Opening
hours: 15 Mar - 30 Jun 10/13 - 15/18, 1
Jul - 31 Aug 10/13 - 15/19, 1 Sep - 15
Nov 10/13 - 15/18, 15 Nov - 31 Dec
10/13.

VILLA BUONVISI (NOW VILLA BOTTINI)
Gardens open to public
Via Elisa   Tel. 0583 / 442140
Opening hours 9/ 13.30

HOTELS

PRINCIPESSA ELISA
S .Statale del Brennero 1952 (3 Km
from Lucca)   Tel. 0583 / 379737

GRAND HOTEL GUINIGI
Via Romana 1247   Tel. 0583 /4991

NAPOLEON
V.le Europa 536   Tel. 0583 / 316516

VILLA LA PRINCIPESSA
S. Statale del Brennero 1616 - Massa Pisana
(3 Km from Lucca)   Tel. 0583 / 370037

VILLA S. MICHELE
Via della Chiesa 462 - S. Michele in
Escheto (4 Km. from Lucca)
Tel. 0583 / 370276

CELIDE
Viale Giusti 25   Tel. 0583 / 954106

LA LUNA
Via Fillungo (corner) Corte Compagni 12   Tel. 0583 / 493634

PICCOLO HOTEL PUCCINI
Via di Poggio 9
Tel. 0583 / 55421 - 53487

REX
Piazza Ricasoli 19
Tel. 0583 / 955443 - 4

San Marco
Via S.Marco 368 - Loc. San Marco
Tel. 0583 / 495010

Universo
Piazza Puccini 1   Tel. 0583 / 493678

Moderno
Via V. Civitali 38   Tel. 0583 / 55840

RESTAURANTS

Antico Caffè delle Mura
Piazza Vittorio Emanuele 2
Tel. 0583 / 47962

Antica Locanda dell'Angelo
Via Pescheria   Tel. 0583 / 47711

Buatino
Via Borgo Giannotti 508   Tel. 0583 / 343207

Buca di S. Antonio
Via della Cervia 3   Tel. 0583 / 55881

Giglio
Piazza del Giglio 2 Tel. 0583 / 494058

Giulio in Pelleria
Via delle Conce 47   Tel. 0583 / 55948

All' Olivo
Piazza S. Quirico 1   Tel. 0583 / 46264

Gli Orti di via Elisa
Via Elisa 17   Tel. 0583 / 491241

Solferino
Via delle Gavine 50 - S. Macario in
Piano   Tel. 0583 / 59118

Teatro
Piazza Napoleone 25   Tel. 0583 / 493740

IN THE VICINITY OF LUCCA
COUNTRY HOUSES

Villa Mansi
Segromigno in Monte   Tel. 0583 / 920234
Closed on Mondays; Opening times
Winter   10/12.30   15/17;   Summer
10/12.30 15/19

Villa Reale Marlia
Tel. 0583 / 30108
Closed on Mondays; Park open 1
Mar - 30 Nov; Visit inside palace by
appointment only

Villa Torrigiani
Camigliano   Tel. 0583 / 928008
Opening times: 1 Mar - 5 Nov 10/12
15/18 (tuesdays closed); In summer-
time 10/13 15/19 – 6 - 30 Nov and
December holidays groups only (
with advance booking)
Closed on Jan and Feb.

HOUSES OF FAMOUS
PERSONALITIES

Puccini's House
Celle Puccini (Pescaglia)   Tel. 0583 / 359154
Opening times: Sat & Sun 15/19
Other days by appointment.

Pascoli's House
Castelvecchio Pascoli   Tel. 0583 / 766147
Closed on Mondays; Opening times

Winter   10/13   14.30/17;   Summer
10/13 15/ 18.30.

MUSEUMS AND PERMANENT
EXHIBITIONS

Barga Museum (Museo Civico del Territorio di Barga)
P.le Arringo - Barga
Tel. 0583 /711100
Closed on Mondays; Opening times:
10.30/12.30 Sun: 10.30/12.30 - 15/17;
Jul & Aug 10.30/12.30 - 16.30/19

Museum of Plaster Figurines and of Emigration
(Museo della figurina di gesso e dell'emigrazione)
Palazzo Vanni - Coreglia Antelminelli
Tel. 0583 / 78082
Closed on Sundays; Opening times
Winter working days: 8/13; Summer
working days: 8/13; Holidays (not
Sundays) 10/13 16/19

Permanent Archaeological Exhibition
Via Vallisneri 8 - Castelnuovo Garfagnana
Opening times: Nov & May Tue 9/13
- 15/18, Fri 9/13

Museum of Ethnographic Exhibition
Capannori Tel. 0583 /935808-935494
Ring for details of opening times of
the various sections.

**Museum of Archaeological Finds
& Renaissance Ceramics**
Inside Castle at Camporgiano (LU)
Tel. 0583 / 618888
apertura a richiesta

NATURE PARKS & TOURIST
ATTRACTIONS NEAR LUCCA

Orecchiella Nature Park
Alta Garfagnana
Open every day in summer months
Tel. 0583 / 619098;
book group visits in other months at:
Amm.ne Foreste Demaniali, Viale
Giusti 65 - Lucca   Tel. 0583 / 955525

Regional Park of Apuan Alps
Information from Visitors Centres in
Castelnuovo Garfagnana
Tel. 0584 / 757361

Botri Gorge
Bagni di Lucca - Fraz. Montefegatesi

Campocatino Nature Park
Vagli Sotto
Information   Tel. 0583 / 664103

Pania di Corfino" Botanical Gardens
Villa Collemandina (inside Orecchiella Park); Guided tours 25 Jun /
10 Sep every day 9 / 12.30 - 14.30 / 18

Wind Grotto (Grotta del vento)
Fornovolasco - Loc. Trimpello
Tel. 0583 /722024
Opening times: 1 Apr/15 Oct every
day guided tours on variable routes;
16 Oct / 31 Mar open only on holi-
days and between Christmas and
New Year's Day with shorter hours.
Groups must book in advance.

INDEX

Photographs: Archivio Plurigraf - Arnaldo Vescovo
Aerial photos authorization S.M.A. n.402 del 16-5-91

© Copyright by CASA EDITRICE PLURIGRAF
S.S. Flaminia, km 90 - 05035 NARNI - TERNI - ITALIA
Tel. 0744 / 715946 - Fax 0744 / 722540 - (Italy country code: +39)
All rights reserved. No Part of this publication may be reproduced.
Printed: 1997 - PLURIGRAF S.p.A. - NARNI

L. 8.000
I.V.A. INCLUSA